SpringerBriefs in Computer Science

AF790233

SpringerBriefs present concise summaries of cutting-edge research and practical applications across a wide spectrum of fields. Featuring compact volumes of 50 to 125 pages, the series covers a range of content from professional to academic.

Typical topics might include:

- A timely report of state-of-the art analytical techniques
- A bridge between new research results, as published in journal articles, and a contextual literature review
- A snapshot of a hot or emerging topic
- An in-depth case study or clinical example
- A presentation of core concepts that students must understand in order to make independent contributions.

Briefs allow authors to present their ideas and readers to absorb them with minimal time investment. Briefs will be published as part of Springer's eBook collection, with millions of users worldwide. In addition, Briefs will be available for individual print and electronic purchase. Briefs are characterized by fast, global electronic dissemination, standard publishing contracts, easy-to-use manuscript preparation and formatting guidelines, and expedited production schedules. We aim for publication 8–12 weeks after acceptance. Both solicited and unsolicited manuscripts are considered for publication in this series.

**Indexing: This series is indexed in Scopus, Ei-Compendex, and zbMATH **

Ran Yi · Zhensheng Li · Wei Zhang

Algorithmic Fairness in AI-Mediated Institutional Communication

A Computational Framework for Multilingual Professional Interaction

Springer

Ran Yi
National University of Defense Technology
Nanjing, Jiangsu, China

Zhensheng Li
Shanghai AI Laboratory
Shanghai, China

Wei Zhang
National University of Defense Technology
Nanjing, Jiangsu, China

ISSN 2191-5768 ISSN 2191-5776 (electronic)
SpringerBriefs in Computer Science
ISBN 978-3-032-28657-4 ISBN 978-3-032-28658-1 (eBook)
https://doi.org/10.1007/978-3-032-28658-1

© The Editor(s) (if applicable) and The Author(s), under exclusive license to Springer Nature Switzerland AG 2026

This work is subject to copyright. All rights are solely and exclusively licensed by the Publisher, whether the whole or part of the material is concerned, specifically the rights of translation, reprinting, reuse of illustrations, recitation, broadcasting, reproduction on microfilms or in any other physical way, and transmission or information storage and retrieval, electronic adaptation, computer software, or by similar or dissimilar methodology now known or hereafter developed.
The use of general descriptive names, registered names, trademarks, service marks, etc. in this publication does not imply, even in the absence of a specific statement, that such names are exempt from the relevant protective laws and regulations and therefore free for general use.
The publisher, the authors and the editors are safe to assume that the advice and information in this book are believed to be true and accurate at the date of publication. Neither the publisher nor the authors or the editors give a warranty, expressed or implied, with respect to the material contained herein or for any errors or omissions that may have been made. The publisher remains neutral with regard to jurisdictional claims in published maps and institutional affiliations.

This Springer imprint is published by the registered company Springer Nature Switzerland AG
The registered company address is: Gewerbestrasse 11, 6330 Cham, Switzerland

If disposing of this product, please recycle the paper.

For my parents—

between a lawyer who sharpened the questions and a judge who weighed the answers, I learned to listen carefully before speaking.

Ran

Preface

What happens when professional communication, particularly communication with legal or institutional consequences, is increasingly mediated by artificial intelligence? How can we ensure that automated language technologies preserve not only the semantic content of speech but also the pragmatic cues that shape interpretation, authority and procedural fairness? And when multilingual communication is involved, how can computational systems avoid amplifying linguistic asymmetries that already exist within institutional environments?

These questions motivated the research presented in this SpringerBrief.

Across courts, regulatory agencies and professional organisations, language technologies are rapidly becoming part of the communicative infrastructure through which decisions are made and information is interpreted. Transformer-based systems and large language models now support tasks ranging from legal document analysis and multilingual translation to summarisation, discourse classification and professional communication assistance. Recent developments in domain-specific AI systems capable of analysing and generating specialised texts further illustrate how computational models increasingly participate in professional knowledge environments. While these advances promise greater efficiency and accessibility, they also introduce new forms of risk. When AI systems participate in institutional communication, even small distortions in meaning, particularly those involving tone, modality or evidentiary stance, can alter how statements are interpreted within procedural contexts.

In this book, we examine these challenges through the lens of algorithmic fairness in AI-mediated institutional communication. Our focus lies on professional environments where language functions not merely as a vehicle for information but as a structured instrument of institutional action. Legal questioning, administrative decision-making and interpreter-mediated communication all rely on carefully calibrated linguistic signals. Discourse markers, hedging expressions, polarity alignment, evidential framing and stance indicators shape how statements function within institutional interactions. When these signals are altered or lost during automated processing, the resulting communication may diverge from its intended institutional meaning.

Despite the rapid progress of natural language processing, evaluation frameworks for AI systems have largely prioritised lexical accuracy and general-domain benchmarks. These metrics are valuable, but they rarely capture the pragmatic and interactional features that define professional discourse. As a result, systems may appear accurate according to conventional benchmarks while quietly degrading the linguistic structures that sustain procedural communication.

Our aim in this Brief is to address this gap by proposing a **computational framework for fairness-aware evaluation in institutional NLP**. Drawing on insights from sociolinguistics, computational linguistics and legal discourse analysis, we develop a methodology that integrates multilingual corpus design, transformer-based benchmarking and discourse-sensitive evaluation metrics. Central to this framework is the **Manner Accuracy Score (MAS 2.0)**, a metric designed to measure not only whether a system predicts correctly but whether it preserves the pragmatic manner in which institutional statements are expressed. In this sense, the framework moves beyond conventional performance metrics by incorporating sociolinguistic indicators of communicative behaviour into computational evaluation.

The methodological design of this framework is informed by developments across several areas of computational research. Advances in AI-driven argument mining and domain-specific language modelling demonstrate how large language models increasingly operate within specialised professional domains. At the same time, research in computational social choice highlights the importance of clearly defined evaluation structures for ensuring fairness and transparency in algorithmic systems that influence institutional decision processes. In parallel, work on manifold learning and model reduction illustrates how complex computational systems can be analysed through structured representations that preserve essential informational properties while enabling systematic evaluation of model behaviour. These complementary perspectives inform the design of the benchmarking architecture developed in this Brief.

The empirical work presented here draws on multilingual institutional datasets that include courtroom questioning patterns and interpreter-mediated communication. These data allow us to examine how pragmatic features such as modality, polarity alignment and discourse markers interact with computational modelling. Through this analysis, we demonstrate that fairness disparities in AI-mediated communication often emerge not through obvious lexical errors but through the gradual degradation of pragmatic signals across languages and institutional contexts.

Importantly, our goal is not to suggest that automated systems should replace human expertise in professional communication. On the contrary, we view computational benchmarking as a tool for accountability and transparency. By identifying where models succeed and where they fall short, fairness-aware evaluation can help institutions deploy language technologies responsibly while maintaining appropriate human oversight.

This work is necessarily interdisciplinary. It draws on methods from natural language processing, corpus linguistics and legal communication studies, reflecting the complexity of institutional language environments. Our hope is that bringing these perspectives together will help advance research at the intersection of computational modelling and professional discourse analysis.

As AI continues to reshape how institutions communicate, the question is no longer whether automated systems will participate in professional discourse, but how they will do so, and under what standards of fairness and accountability. We hope this Brief contributes to that conversation by offering a framework for evaluating linguistic equity in multilingual institutional communication systems and by encouraging further collaboration across disciplines concerned with language, technology and justice.

Nanjing, China — Ran Yi
Shanghai, China — Zhensheng Li
Nanjing, China — Wei Zhang

Acknowledgements This project has benefited from the support, expertise and generosity of many colleagues across disciplines. We are deeply grateful to the judges, lawyers, judicial officers, interpreters and computer scientists who shared their time, professional insight and experience. Their perspectives helped ensure that the computational models developed in this study remain grounded in the practical realities of institutional communication.

We would also like to thank **Dr. Alexandru Ciolan**, whose editorial guidance and thoughtful engagement greatly supported the development of this book.

Part of the empirical material used in this research was drawn from interpreter-mediated bilingual trials approved by the **UNSW Human Research Ethics Committee (HC210787)**. All participants provided informed consent. Some experimental materials were derived from the **Australian Research Council Discovery Project (DP180100124)** and are used with the consent of the chief investigators and the individuals involved.

This study was supported by **UNSW Sydney (HAL SPF02) and in part by the National University of Defense Technology (NUDT) Faculty Startup Fund**. We gratefully acknowledge this support.

Finally, we thank our colleagues and collaborators who contributed discussions, feedback and intellectual encouragement during the development of this work.

Competing Interests The authors have no competing interests to declare that are relevant to the content of this manuscript.

Contents

Chapter 1
Introduction: Fairness in AI-Mediated Institutional Communication

Keywords AI-mediated communication · Institutional discourse · Multilingual NLP · Algorithmic fairness · Professional communication systems · Transformer-based language models

1.1 Introduction

Artificial intelligence increasingly mediates communication in institutional settings. In legal systems, administrative procedures, and professional decision-making environments, language technologies now assist or shape interactions that previously depended entirely on human discourse. Large Language Models (LLMs) and transformer-based architectures have become central components of this infrastructure, supporting tasks such as legal document analysis, translation, summarisation, and decision support [1, 2]. Earlier work on representation learning and domain-specific language modelling has also demonstrated how neural architectures can capture both local semantic relations and global textual structure in classification tasks, providing foundational insights for downstream institutional language processing [3]. These systems are rapidly entering domains where linguistic accuracy and procedural legitimacy are tightly intertwined. As a result, questions of fairness in AI-mediated communication have become both technically and institutionally significant.

Existing research on fairness in natural language processing has primarily focused on demographic bias. Studies commonly examine disparities in sentiment classification, toxicity detection, or representation of demographic groups in language models. While this work has produced important methodological advances, it has concentrated largely on general-domain language use. Research across related machine learning domains, including medical imaging and biomedical signal classification, illustrates how model design and sequential feature integration can substantially

© The Author(s), under exclusive license to Springer Nature Switzerland AG 2026

R. Yi et al., *Algorithmic Fairness in AI-Mediated Institutional Communication*, SpringerBriefs in Computer Science, https://doi.org/10.1007/978-3-032-28658-1_1

influence system performance and interpretability, highlighting the broader methodological challenges involved in ensuring reliable and equitable model behaviour across specialised domains [4, 5]. By contrast, professional discourse, particularly legal or administrative communication, has received comparatively little attention within fairness-oriented NLP research. This gap is consequential because institutional discourse operates under conditions where linguistic errors do not merely distort meaning; they can affect credibility, procedural rights, and decision outcomes.

The present study addresses this gap by examining fairness in multilingual institutional communication systems. Specifically, it investigates how AI-assisted language technologies interact with structured legal discourse, focusing on courtroom questioning and interpreter-mediated communication. The analysis integrates computational modelling with discourse-analytic methods to examine how linguistic structure, pragmatic tone, and institutional asymmetry jointly shape fairness outcomes. Prior interdisciplinary research has shown that cultural information environments and linguistic practices shape how technology-mediated communication is interpreted within institutional contexts, underscoring the importance of examining language technologies within their broader sociocultural and informational frameworks [6]. By doing so, the study contributes to an emerging research agenda that connects computational linguistics with legal discourse analysis and procedural justice.

1.2 Institutional Discourse and Procedural Communication

Institutional communication differs fundamentally from everyday conversation. In professional environments such as courts, regulatory hearings, or administrative proceedings, language is governed by formal procedures and normative constraints [7–9]. Participants occupy defined roles, and their speech acts carry legally or administratively consequential implications. Linguistic choices therefore operate within a system of accountability that shapes how statements are interpreted and evaluated.

Within legal contexts, this structured communication is particularly visible. Courtroom discourse is organized through institutional turn-taking rules, evidentiary constraints, and adversarial questioning practices [10, 11]. Lawyers, judges, witnesses, and interpreters each perform role-specific communicative functions. These interactions are not merely exchanges of information; they are mechanisms through which legal arguments are constructed and evaluated.

A key characteristic of institutional discourse is that linguistic form often functions strategically. Question design, clause structure, and pragmatic markers can influence how participants respond and how their responses are interpreted. For instance, tag questions in courtroom cross-examination frequently operate as confirmatory devices that constrain possible answers while appearing to invite agreement. Linguistic features therefore become tools through which institutional authority and epistemic control are exercised.

These dynamics become even more complex in multilingual settings. When courtroom communication is mediated through interpreters, the linguistic structure of questions and responses interacts with cross-linguistic differences and cognitive constraints. Interpreters must simultaneously preserve semantic content, pragmatic intent, and procedural accuracy. Under such conditions, subtle linguistic cues, such as discourse markers or hedging expressions, may be altered or omitted. These changes can affect how statements are perceived by judges or juries, thereby influencing the procedural fairness of the interaction [7, 12, 13].

1.3 Fairness in AI-Mediated Professional Communication

As AI systems increasingly process and analyse institutional language, fairness considerations extend beyond demographic bias to include discourse-level reliability and procedural integrity. In professional environments, fairness is closely tied to whether linguistic representations preserve the communicative intentions and institutional roles embedded in the original interaction.

Traditional fairness metrics in machine learning typically focus on statistical parity across demographic groups. However, institutional discourse raises additional dimensions of fairness. Errors in professional language processing may alter the pragmatic force of statements, misrepresent speaker intent, or distort the evidentiary structure of an interaction. In legal settings, such distortions can have direct implications for procedural justice.

For example, courtroom questioning often relies on nuanced linguistic cues to establish credibility or challenge testimony. If an AI-supported system, such as automated transcription, translation, or sentiment analysis, fails to capture these cues, it may misrepresent the interactional dynamics of the exchange. This is particularly relevant in multilingual proceedings where interpreters already face cognitive constraints and linguistic asymmetries.

Recent developments in transformer-based models have significantly improved the performance of NLP systems across tasks such as translation, classification, and semantic representation [14]. Nevertheless, these models are typically trained on large general-language corpora that do not reflect the structural characteristics of institutional discourse. As a result, the models may lack sensitivity to domain-specific pragmatic signals, such as those embedded in courtroom questioning or professional negotiation.

Consequently, fairness in institutional NLP systems must be evaluated not only through aggregate accuracy metrics but also through their ability to preserve discourse-level functions. This study therefore adopts a broader conceptualisation of fairness that incorporates linguistic, computational, and institutional dimensions.

1.4 A Three-Layer Model of Fairness in Institutional NLP

To operationalise fairness in professional communication systems, this book proposes a three-layer analytical framework. Each layer corresponds to a different level at which fairness may be compromised or preserved in AI-mediated institutional communication.

Discourse-Level Pragmatic Competence

The first layer concerns the linguistic structure of institutional discourse itself. Professional communication relies heavily on pragmatic cues such as stance markers, modality, polarity alignment, and discourse markers. These elements signal speaker intent, epistemic commitment, and interactional pressure.

For example, in courtroom cross-examination, tag questions with polarity reversal often function as confirmatory assertions rather than genuine inquiries. When combined with epistemic downtoners or modal auxiliaries, these constructions shape the interactional dynamics between lawyers and witnesses. Computational models must therefore capture not only lexical content but also these pragmatic configurations.

Failure to detect such structures may lead to incorrect interpretation of discourse functions. For instance, a question that appears syntactically neutral may in fact function as a coercive assertion. Accurate modelling of institutional discourse therefore requires systems capable of recognising these pragmatic patterns.

Model-Level Performance Parity

The second layer addresses fairness at the level of computational models. Machine learning systems must perform consistently across linguistic contexts and interactional conditions. In multilingual legal settings, this includes maintaining comparable performance across languages, discourse types, and interpretation modes.

Performance disparities may arise from several sources. Training datasets may lack domain-specific examples, leading to reduced accuracy when models encounter institutional language patterns. Similarly, multilingual models may exhibit asymmetries in how they process pragmatically complex constructions across languages.

Model-level fairness therefore involves evaluating classification accuracy, recall, and error patterns across different discourse conditions. By analysing how models perform on specific linguistic features, such as polarity alignment or modal softening, it becomes possible to identify systematic biases in model behaviour.

System-Level Accountability Alignment

The third layer concerns the institutional deployment of AI systems. Even when individual models perform well in controlled settings, their integration into real-world decision-making processes introduces additional fairness challenges.

Institutional systems must ensure transparency, interpretability, and accountability. This is particularly important in legal contexts, where automated analyses may influence procedural decisions or evidentiary interpretation. Model outputs must therefore be interpretable by legal professionals and open to scrutiny.

Explainable AI techniques provide tools for addressing this requirement. Feature attribution methods, such as permutation importance or Shapley-based explanations, allow researchers to identify which linguistic features drive model predictions. By linking computational outputs to theoretically motivated linguistic categories, these methods enhance the transparency of AI-assisted analysis.

1.5 Empirical Context of the Study

The empirical analysis presented in this book draws on two complementary datasets. The first consists of a corpus of prosecutorial questioning extracted from legally vetted trial scripts and annotated for discourse function. This dataset enables the computational modelling of morphosyntactic patterns associated with coercive and cooperative questioning strategies.

The second dataset originates from a bilingual courtroom experiment involving interpreter-mediated communication in remote settings. The original recordings comprise approximately 3250 min of interpreted criminal trial simulations. These recordings were transcribed and annotated for sentiment, pragmatic tone, and interpreter errors.

Combining these datasets allows the study to examine fairness in institutional communication from two perspectives. The first focuses on the linguistic design of courtroom questioning, analyzing how morphosyntactic configurations encode interactional pressure. The second examines how this discourse features interact with multilingual interpretation, particularly in relation to sentiment shifts and interpreter errors. Together, these analyses provide a comprehensive view of how institutional language patterns propagate through AI-mediated communication systems.

1.6 Methodological Roadmap

The methodological approach adopted in this book integrates corpus linguistics, computational modelling, and discourse analysis. The analytical pipeline proceeds through several stages.

First, linguistically motivated feature families are extracted from annotated corpora. These features include polarity alignment, modal auxiliaries, epistemic markers, and discourse markers. Dependency parsing and feature engineering techniques are used to operationalize these categories computationally.

Second, supervised machine learning models are applied to classify discourse functions and predict interpreter errors. Ensemble methods and transformer-based models are evaluated using cross-validation procedures and standard performance metrics such as precision, recall, and F1 score [15].

Third, explainability techniques are employed to interpret model behaviors. Feature attribution analyses identify which linguistic cues most strongly influence model predictions. These results are then interpreted within a discourse-analytic framework informed by sociolinguistic and legal discourse research.

This combination of quantitative modelling and qualitative interpretation reflects a mixed-method research design. The approach enables computational findings to be contextualized within broader theories of institutional language use.

1.7 Fairness in Multilingual Institutional Contexts

Multilingual communication introduces additional complexity into fairness evaluation. Legal discourse often involves participants with varying levels of linguistic proficiency. When interpretation is required, communicative accuracy depends not only on linguistic equivalence but also on the preservation of pragmatic tone and discourse structure.

Research on courtroom interpreting has demonstrated that interpreters frequently face trade-offs between semantic accuracy and pragmatic fidelity [16, 17]. Under conditions of cognitive load, such as rapid cross-examination or emotionally charged questioning, interpreters may omit discourse markers or modify hedging expressions. These changes can alter the perceived intent of the original utterance.

AI-based language technologies interact with these dynamics in two ways. On the one hand, they can assist interpreters by identifying pragmatic cues and highlighting potential errors. On the other hand, poorly calibrated models may amplify existing asymmetries by misclassifying discourse features or failing to detect sentiment shifts.

Evaluating fairness in such systems therefore requires attention to both computational performance and institutional consequences. Systems must be assessed not only for overall accuracy but also for their impact on communication equity among participants.

1.8 Contribution of This Study

This book contributes to the emerging field of fairness-aware institutional NLP in several ways.

First, it introduces a conceptual framework that integrates discourse analysis with fairness-aware machine learning. By distinguishing discourse-level, model-level, and system-level dimensions of fairness, the framework provides a structured approach to evaluating AI-mediated communication systems.

Second, the study demonstrates how morphosyntactic features of institutional discourse can be operationalized within computational models. The analysis shows that interactional phenomena such as coercive questioning are systematically encoded in linguistic form and can be detected using machine learning techniques.

Third, the research expands fairness evaluation into multilingual legal contexts. By combining courtroom discourse analysis with interpreter-mediated communication data, the study highlights how linguistic asymmetries and computational systems jointly shape procedural outcomes.

Finally, the methodological approach illustrates how mixed methods can bridge computational modelling and qualitative discourse analysis. This integration enhances both interpretability and practical relevance for institutional stakeholders.

1.9 Structure of the Brief

The remainder of this Brief develops the conceptual and empirical foundations outlined in this chapter.

Subsequent chapters first review representation learning and transfer learning techniques relevant to legal NLP. These chapters explain how transformer-based architectures and feature engineering methods can be adapted to domain-specific discourse analysis.

Later chapters present the empirical analyses of courtroom questioning and interpreter-mediated communication. These sections examine morphosyntactic predictors of coerciveness, sentiment shifts in bilingual discourse, and machine learning models for predicting interpretation errors.

The final chapters discuss the implications of these findings for fairness evaluation in AI-mediated institutional communication. Particular attention is given to interpretability, accountability, and the design of fairness-aware benchmarking frameworks.

By integrating computational methods with discourse analysis, the study seeks to advance a more domain-sensitive approach to fairness in natural language processing. Such an approach is essential for ensuring that AI systems support, not undermine, the procedural integrity of institutional communication.

References

1. Devlin, J., Chang, M.-W., Lee, K., Toutanova, K.: BERT: Pre-training of deep bidirectional transformers for language understanding. In: Proceedings of NAACL 2019. Association for Computational Linguistics, pp 4171–4186 (2019). https://doi.org/10.18653/v1/N19-1423
2. Vaswani, A., Shazeer, N., Parmar, N., Uszkoreit, J., Jones, L., Gomez, A.N., Kaiser, Ł., Polosukhin, I.: Attention is all you need. In: Advances in Neural Information Processing Systems, pp. 5998–6008, 2017. URL https://proceedings.neurips.cc/paper/2017/hash/3f5ee243547dee91fbd053c1c4a845aa-Abstract.html.
3. Zhao, J., Zhan, Z., Yang, Q., Zhang, Y., Hu, C., Li, Z., He, Z.: Adaptive learning of local semantic and global structure representations for text classification. In: Proceedings of COLING 2018, pp. 2033–2043. Association for Computational Linguistics (2018). URL https://aclanthology.org/C18-1173/.

4. Li, Y., Zhang, Y., Liu, C., Li, Z., Li, J., He, Z.: Combining convolutional neural network and distance distribution matrix for identification of congestive heart failure. IEEE Access **6**, 39734–39741 (2018). https://doi.org/10.1109/ACCESS.2018.2855420
5. Zhang, Y., Jiang, X., Zhong, C., Zhang, Y., Shi, Z., Li, Z., He, Z.: SequentialSegNet: combination with sequential feature for multi-organ segmentation. In Proceedings of ICPR 2018, pp. 3947–3952. IEEE (2018). URL https://ieeexplore.ieee.org/document/8546017
6. Chen, L., Zhang, X., Li, Z.: Understanding the Chinese information culture and its impact on IT perceptions. Inf. Technol. People **33**(1), 56–82 (2020). https://doi.org/10.1108/ITP-03-2018-0128
7. Yi, R.: Justice under the microscope: analyzing Mandarin Chinese markers in virtual courtroom discourse. Discourse Stud. **26**(1), 117–135 (2024). https://doi.org/10.1177/14614456231197045
8. Yi, R.: Tech-empowered equity: advancing linguistic justice through digital scholarship. Digit. Scholarsh. Human. **40**, 381–399 (2025). https://doi.org/10.1093/llc/fqaf007
9. Yi, R.: Enhancing sentiment analysis and error prediction in lawyer questioning through legal NLP models: a mixed methods study in Australian courtrooms. J. Mixed Meth. Res. (2026). https://doi.org/10.1177/15586898261429189
10. Gibbons, J.: Forensic Linguistics: An Introduction to Language in the Justice System. Blackwell (2003)
11. Solan, L.M., Tiersma, P.M.: Speaking of Crime: The Language of Criminal Justice. University of Chicago Press (2005)
12. Berk-Seligson, S.: The bilingual courtroom: court interpreters in the judicial process, 2nd edn. University of Chicago Press (2017)
13. Hale, S.B.: The Discourse of Court Interpreting: Discourse Practices of the Law, the Witness, and the Interpreter. John Benjamins (2004)
14. Jurafsky, D., Martin, J.H.: Speech and language processing, 3rd edn (draft). Pearson (2021)
15. Hastie, T., Tibshirani, R., Friedman, J.: The Elements of Statistical Learning: Data Mining, Inference, and Prediction, 2nd edn. Springer (2009)
16. Hale, S.B.: Community Interpreting. Palgrave Macmillan (2007)
17. Liu, X.: Pragmalinguistic challenges for trainee interpreters in achieving accuracy. Interpreting **22**(1), 87–116 (2020). https://doi.org/10.1075/intp.00035.liu

Chapter 2
Theoretical Foundations: From Sociolinguistics to Computational Fairness

Keywords Computational sociolinguistics · Linguistic equity · Fairness metrics in NLP · Pragmatic competence modelling · Discourse-aware evaluation · Manner Accuracy Score (MAS)

2.1 Introduction

The growing integration of artificial intelligence into institutional communication systems raises fundamental questions about linguistic equity. In professional environments such as courts, regulatory hearings, and administrative procedures, communication is not simply informational exchange. It is a structured process governed by procedural norms, evidentiary standards, and interactional conventions. Consequently, fairness in AI-mediated institutional communication must account for how language functions within these structured environments.

This chapter develops the theoretical foundations necessary to operationalise linguistic equity in computational systems. It translates core sociolinguistic concepts, pragmatic appropriateness, discourse alignment, and communicative accountability, into measurable constructs suitable for computational modelling. Building on research in sociolinguistics, discourse analysis, and fairness-aware machine learning, the chapter proposes a framework that connects linguistic theory with quantitative evaluation.

The discussion proceeds in four stages. First, we examine the role of pragmatic and interactional structures in institutional communication. Second, we review existing fairness metrics in machine learning and assess their limitations for discourse-sensitive applications. Third, we introduce the concept of linguistic equity as a measurable property of multilingual NLP systems. Finally, we present the theoretical foundations for a discourse-aware evaluation metric, the **Manner Accuracy Score (MAS 2.0)**, designed to quantify pragmatic fidelity in multilingual outputs.

© The Author(s), under exclusive license to Springer Nature Switzerland AG 2026

R. Yi et al., *Algorithmic Fairness in AI-Mediated Institutional Communication*, SpringerBriefs in Computer Science, https://doi.org/10.1007/978-3-032-28658-1_2

2.2 Institutional Communication as Regulated Discourse

Institutional communication differs from everyday conversation in both structure and purpose. In professional environments, linguistic interaction occurs within formally defined procedures that regulate participation, authority, and evidentiary relevance. These constraints shape not only what participants say but also how their statements are interpreted.

In legal settings, for example, courtroom discourse is governed by rules of procedure that structure the flow of communication. Lawyers question witnesses under strict evidentiary conditions, judges regulate turn-taking, and interpreters mediate communication between participants who do not share a common language [1, 2]. Within this system, linguistic form carries institutional consequences. The phrasing of a question, the use of modal verbs, or the presence of discourse markers may influence how testimony is perceived and evaluated.

Three characteristics distinguish institutional discourse from general conversational interaction.

Regulated Turn-Taking

Institutional communication relies on regulated participation structures. Unlike everyday conversation, where turn-taking is negotiated dynamically, institutional settings assign communicative roles. In courtroom proceedings, lawyers ask questions, witnesses provide answers, and judges intervene to maintain procedural order. Each role carries specific constraints on permissible speech acts.

These constraints shape the design of utterances. For instance, cross-examination questions often take the form of declarative statements followed by confirmatory tags. This structure narrows the range of acceptable responses and places epistemic pressure on the respondent. Linguistic choices therefore function as tools for managing interactional authority.

Evidentiary Precision

A second defining feature of institutional discourse is its emphasis on evidentiary precision. Statements made in legal or administrative contexts may carry formal consequences, including legal liability or procedural decisions. As a result, linguistic ambiguity can have significant implications.

Participants often rely on specific grammatical constructions to calibrate evidentiary commitment. Modal verbs such as *may* or *might* signal uncertainty, while hedging expressions such as *I believe* or *it appears* reduce the strength of an assertion. Conversely, categorical statements or confirmatory tags may signal high epistemic certainty.

Automated language systems must therefore recognise these distinctions. If computational models fail to capture evidentiary nuance, they risk misrepresenting the strength or intent of a statement.

Mitigation and Pragmatic Calibration

Institutional discourse also relies heavily on pragmatic mitigation strategies. Speakers frequently employ linguistic devices, such as discourse markers, hedges, and modal auxiliaries, to manage interpersonal relations and regulate the force of their statements.

These features are particularly important in adversarial settings such as courtroom questioning. Lawyers may combine assertive statements with pragmatic softening devices to balance institutional authority with procedural expectations of fairness. For example, a question such as *"You didn't think it was necessary to report the incident, did you?"* simultaneously asserts a claim and invites confirmation.

Such constructions illustrate how pragmatic calibration operates within institutional communication. Linguistic form is carefully designed to project particular interactional outcomes while maintaining procedural legitimacy.

2.3 Distortion Risks in Automated Language Systems

As NLP systems increasingly analyse and generate institutional language, the risk of discourse distortion becomes a critical concern. Transformer-based models have demonstrated impressive performance across many language tasks [3, 4]. However, these models are typically trained on large general-domain corpora rather than specialised institutional discourse.

This mismatch between training data and deployment context can produce several types of distortion.

Pragmatic Signal Loss

Automated systems often prioritise lexical content over pragmatic structure. As a result, discourse markers, hedging expressions, or stance indicators may be ignored or misinterpreted. In multilingual contexts, translation systems may omit these markers entirely, altering the perceived tone or intent of the original utterance.

For example, discourse markers such as *so*, *well*, or *now* frequently function as pragmatic anchors in courtroom questioning. Their omission in automated translation or interpretation may neutralise the rhetorical force of a question.

Sentiment Misclassification

Sentiment analysis models typically classify utterances according to polarity categories such as positive, negative, or neutral. While such classifications are effective for many applications, they can be inadequate when applied to institutional discourse such as courtroom interaction. In adversarial legal settings, linguistic form frequently performs strategic procedural functions rather than expressing personal affect. Consequently, treating sentiment as a proxy for speaker attitude can lead to systematic misinterpretation of legally significant language patterns.

Recent advances in legal NLP have been driven by large annotated datasets designed for tasks such as legal question answering, classification, and judgment prediction [5–7]. Benchmarks such as LexGLUE and related shared tasks have enabled substantial progress in modelling doctrinal reasoning and document-level inference [8, 9]. However, surveys of the field consistently note that most datasets treat legal language as static textual content rather than as situated interaction [10]. As a result, conversational dynamics and pragmatic features that shape courtroom outcomes remain largely underrepresented in training corpora.

Sentiment misclassification becomes particularly salient in adversarial questioning. Prosecutorial questions often adopt a skeptical, confrontational, or negatively framed tone in order to constrain testimony and manage epistemic authority. These forms may superficially resemble negative sentiment but function instead as institutional tools for structuring responses and testing credibility. Empirical studies in discourse analysis demonstrate that grammatical design, such as polarity alignment, presupposition triggers, and modality selection, plays a central role in shaping how answers are produced and interpreted in legal settings [11, 12]. When NLP models interpret such structures purely as expressions of negative sentiment, they risk misrepresenting the procedural role of questioning.

This limitation reflects a broader methodological issue in legal NLP. Many widely used datasets emphasize doctrinal reasoning tasks while abstracting away from interactional form [10, 13]. Consequently, models trained on these resources may perform well on document-centric benchmarks yet fail to capture interaction-level signals that are critical in courtroom discourse. Research on legal language understanding increasingly highlights the need to incorporate pragmatic and discourse features into computational representations of legal communication [14].

Cross-Linguistic Asymmetry

Cross-linguistic processing introduces an additional layer of complexity. Multilingual legal NLP systems must account for structural differences between languages that influence how stance, mitigation, and epistemic commitment are expressed. While multilingual corpora have expanded rapidly, enabling cross-jurisdictional modelling of legal texts [15, 16], pragmatic equivalence across languages remains difficult to achieve. Linguistic structures that function as hedges or mitigators in one language may be rendered more assertively in another due to grammatical or discourse conventions.

This asymmetry is particularly consequential in interpreter-mediated proceedings. Courtroom interpreting requires the rapid transformation of questions and responses across languages while preserving procedural intent. Research on courtroom discourse shows that subtle shifts in grammatical form can alter the perceived stance or authority of a question [17]. For example, hedging expressions that soften prosecutorial questions in English may be translated into structurally stronger statements in another language, inadvertently increasing the perceived level of assertion. Such shifts can influence how participants evaluate credibility and how witnesses understand their obligations during questioning.

The rise of technology-mediated hearings further amplifies these challenges. Virtual court environments modify communicative cues such as prosody, turn-taking, and audio quality, which can affect how utterances are interpreted [18]. These changes interact with linguistic structure in ways that may not be captured by standard sentiment analysis models. When automated systems process transcripts from such environments without accounting for interactional context, they may misclassify strategically designed legal language as emotional expression.

Addressing these issues requires moving beyond traditional sentiment classification frameworks toward models that capture the interactional and institutional functions of language. Recent work in legal NLP emphasizes the importance of incorporating discourse-level annotations that encode pragmatic features such as epistemic stance, presupposition, and response constraint [19]. By modelling how grammatical structures shape interaction rather than merely identifying lexical sentiment, such approaches provide a more accurate representation of courtroom communication.

In this context, fairness evaluation for institutional NLP systems must extend beyond conventional performance metrics. Accuracy, precision, and recall may conceal systematic misinterpretations if models fail to represent the pragmatic functions of legal language. A system that correctly identifies sentiment polarity but misinterprets adversarial questioning as emotional hostility may still introduce distortions in downstream applications such as credibility assessment, dialogue classification, or automated legal analytics. Ensuring equitable and reliable legal NLP therefore requires datasets and evaluation frameworks that reflect the interactional realities of institutional discourse.

2.4 Fairness Metrics in Machine Learning

Fairness research in machine learning has produced a wide range of quantitative metrics for evaluating whether model behaviour differs systematically across protected groups. These metrics are now widely used in high-stakes domains such as lending, hiring, healthcare, education, and criminal justice, but the literature also shows that no single metric is universally appropriate; rather, the choice of metric depends on the task, the decision context, the harm model, and the underlying distribution of outcomes [20, 21]. This point is especially important in legal and institutional NLP, where concerns about fairness arise not only from prediction error, but also from how linguistic phenomena are represented, abstracted, or normalised during modelling [10, 22].

Three widely discussed group-based fairness metrics are particularly relevant in this context: demographic parity, equalised odds, and calibration. They provide useful but partial perspectives on bias, because they operationalise fairness at the level of statistical outputs rather than at the level of discourse function or pragmatic meaning [23, 24].

Demographic Parity

Demographic parity requires that model predictions be statistically independent of protected attributes such as gender, race, or language background. In binary classification, this means that the probability of receiving a positive prediction should be equal across groups, regardless of group membership [20, 21]. The metric is attractive because it is simple, transparent, and effective for detecting disparities in outcome allocation, and it has therefore been widely used in fairness audits of automated decision systems. However, demographic parity can be too coarse in settings where outcome base rates differ across groups, because equalising positive prediction rates may obscure important differences between legitimate variation in the target distribution and unfair model behaviour [23, 24]. In institutional discourse analysis, this limitation is particularly salient: linguistic asymmetries across speakers or settings may reflect genre, role, or procedural structure rather than discrimination per se. A demographic-parity analysis can therefore reveal distributional imbalance, but it cannot by itself determine whether the model is treating linguistically situated behaviour unfairly [10, 22].

Equalised Odds

The equalised odds criterion requires that a model achieve comparable true-positive rates and false-positive rates across protected groups conditional on the ground-truth label [23]. Unlike demographic parity, this method evaluates fairness in relation to predictive error, and it is therefore often regarded as more appropriate when the goal is to compare model performance rather than raw outcome allocation [20, 21]. For this reason, equalised odds has been especially influential in discussions of high-stakes classification, where unequal error rates may distribute institutional burdens unevenly across groups. Even so, the metric still rests on an outcome-based conception of fairness. It asks whether the model makes mistakes at similar rates across groups, but not whether it represents the linguistic signal itself in an equivalent or contextually faithful way. In legal discourse, that distinction matters: a model may satisfy equalised odds numerically while still encoding courtroom scepticism, mitigation, stance, or coercive questioning as if these were simple sentiment-bearing features [19, 22]. Thus, equalised odds is valuable for auditing predictive parity in error patterns, but insufficient for evaluating whether institutional language has been modelled in a pragmatically adequate manner [10].

Calibration

Calibration measures whether predicted probabilities correspond to observed outcome frequencies across groups. A calibrated model assigns the same empirical meaning to a given score regardless of group membership. For example, a prediction score of 0.8 should correspond to approximately the same observed event rate in each group [24]. This notion is particularly important in risk scoring and probabilistic decision support, because it concerns the reliability and interpretability of model confidence rather than only binary accuracy. At the same time, foundational work on algorithmic fairness shows that calibration can come into tension with other fairness criteria, especially when groups differ in base rates, making simultaneous satisfaction of multiple metrics difficult or impossible in many realistic settings [24]. For institutional NLP, calibration helps assess whether model scores are comparably trustworthy across groups, but it still does not reveal whether the model has captured discourse-pragmatic features consistently across legal, linguistic, or cross-cultural contexts. In other words, a model can be well calibrated and yet still misrepresent the institutional function of hedging, challenge, mitigation, or epistemic positioning in courtroom interaction [22, 25].

These metrics remain indispensable for bias evaluation, but they are not sufficient on their own for fairness assessment in institutional language technologies. They quantify disparities in outputs, errors, or probabilities. They do not directly test whether models preserve the pragmatic and interactional meaning of discourse across speakers, languages, and procedural settings. For that reason, fairness analysis in legal NLP should combine standard statistical metrics with discourse-sensitive evaluation frameworks that examine representational adequacy, contextual validity, and the risk of functionally distorted language modelling [10, 22, 25].

2.5 Limitations of Traditional Fairness Metrics

Although these metrics provide valuable tools for assessing algorithmic bias, they have significant limitations when applied to multilingual institutional discourse.

First, traditional fairness metrics focus primarily on demographic attributes rather than linguistic structures. In institutional communication, fairness may depend more on the preservation of pragmatic meaning than on demographic representation. For example, in courtroom questioning a prosecutor may ask a negatively framed confirmatory question such as "You didn't see the defendant that night, did you?" Although the surface polarity of the utterance may appear negative, its institutional function is to constrain the range of acceptable responses and test evidential consistency. A sentiment-based model that interprets the utterance as expressing negative emotion would misrepresent the interactional intent. Demographic parity could still be satisfied, because the model's predictions might not differ across demographic groups, yet the linguistic structure that encodes procedural pressure would remain unrecognised. In such cases, fairness concerns arise not from demographic imbalance but from the model's inability to represent the pragmatic force of the question.

Second, these metrics evaluate prediction outcomes without considering how linguistic information is encoded within the model. Two systems may produce similar classification accuracy while differing significantly in their treatment of pragmatic cues. For instance, two dialogue classification systems may both achieve high accuracy in identifying "challenging" or "neutral" questions in courtroom transcripts. However, one system might rely primarily on lexical sentiment cues (e.g., negative adjectives or evaluative verbs), while another incorporates syntactic patterns such as polarity alignment, modal restriction, or presupposition triggers. Although the overall performance metrics appear equivalent, the first model may systematically misinterpret legally routine adversarial questioning as emotional hostility, whereas the second captures the structural features that signal institutional challenge. Traditional fairness metrics would treat these models as comparable because their prediction outcomes are similar, even though their internal linguistic representations differ substantially.

Third, fairness metrics designed for static datasets may not account for interactional dynamics. Institutional discourse often involves sequential exchanges in which meaning emerges through interaction rather than isolated statements. A witness examination illustrates this problem. A prosecutor may begin with an apparently neutral question ("You arrived at the house at 8 pm?"), followed by a sequence of increasingly constrained confirmatory questions that progressively narrow the witness's response options. Each individual utterance may appear linguistically neutral when analysed in isolation. However, the coercive or directive effect emerges across the sequence of turns, where earlier answers shape the interpretation of later questions. A model evaluated only on sentence-level predictions might satisfy fairness metrics across demographic groups while still failing to capture this sequential pressure. Consequently, fairness assessment based solely on static utterance classification overlooks the interactional processes through which institutional meaning is constructed.

Consequently, evaluating fairness in institutional NLP requires metrics capable of capturing discourse-level variation. Such evaluation should consider not only statistical parity across groups but also whether models preserve pragmatic meaning, structural constraints on responses, and the sequential organisation of institutional interaction.

2.6 Defining Linguistic Equity

To address these limitations, this study introduces the concept of **linguistic equity**. Linguistic equity refers to the degree to which computational systems preserve the functional properties of language across linguistic groups, discourse types, and communicative contexts.

Formally, linguistic equity can be understood as the absence of systematic performance variance across language conditions when controlling for discourse function.

Let:

P represent model performance on a specific discourse task,
L represent language or language group,
D represent discourse function.

A system exhibits linguistic equity if performance differences across language groups remain within an acceptable tolerance threshold when evaluated for the same discourse function

$$\left|P(L_i, D) - P\left(L_j, D\right)\right| \leq \varepsilon$$

where ϵ represents the acceptable variance threshold.

This definition emphasises that fairness in institutional NLP involves maintaining consistent interpretive accuracy across languages and discourse structures.

2.7 Pragmatic Feature Retention

One practical way to evaluate linguistic equity is through **pragmatic feature retention**. Institutional discourse relies heavily on features such as: discourse markers, modal auxiliaries, hedging expressions, polarity alignment, and stance markers.

If these features are systematically lost or altered in automated outputs, the resulting discourse may misrepresent the speaker's communicative intent.

Pragmatic feature retention measures the proportion of such features preserved during computational processing.

Let:

F_o represent the number of pragmatic features in the original utterance,
F_r represent the number retained in the processed output.

Retention rate can be expressed as:

$$R = \frac{F_r}{F_o}$$

Lower retention rates indicate greater pragmatic distortion.

2.8 Error Distribution Differentials

A second indicator of linguistic inequity is **error distribution differential**. Even when overall model accuracy appears high, errors may cluster in specific discourse contexts.

For example, a system may perform well on neutral statements but struggle with questions containing stance markers or complex modality. If these contexts disproportionately affect particular language groups, the system may produce unequal communicative outcomes.

Error distribution differential can therefore be measured by comparing error rates across discourse categories:

$$\Delta E = E_{\text{context},1} - E_{\text{context},2}$$

Large differentials suggest that the system performs unevenly across discourse structures.

2.9 The Manner Accuracy Score (MAS 2.0)

Building on these principles, this study introduces the **Manner Accuracy Score (MAS 2.0)** as a metric for evaluating pragmatic fidelity in multilingual NLP systems.

MAS 2.0 extends traditional accuracy measures by incorporating discourse-level information. The metric evaluates whether computational outputs preserve the pragmatic manner in which statements are expressed, rather than only their propositional content.

The score integrates three components:

Semantic Accuracy
Measures whether the propositional content of the output matches the source.

Pragmatic Feature Retention
Evaluates whether discourse markers, modality, and stance indicators are preserved.

Discourse Function Consistency
Assesses whether the interactional role of the utterance, such as coercive questioning or cooperative inquiry, remains intact.

Formally:

$$\text{MAS} = \alpha S + \beta R + \gamma D$$

where:

S = semantic accuracy
R = pragmatic feature retention
D = discourse function consistency
α, β, γ = weighting coefficients.

MAS 2.0 therefore captures both linguistic fidelity and discourse-level fairness.

2.10 From Theory to Computational Evaluation

The theoretical framework developed in this chapter provides the foundation for the computational analyses presented in later chapters. By linking sociolinguistic concepts with measurable computational constructs, the framework enables systematic evaluation of fairness in AI-mediated institutional communication.

Three key principles guide this evaluation.

First, fairness must be assessed at the level of discourse structure rather than solely through demographic metrics. Institutional communication relies on pragmatic features that conventional fairness metrics do not capture.

Second, multilingual systems must be evaluated for their ability to preserve pragmatic meaning across languages. Cross-linguistic variation should not produce systematic distortions in communicative intent.

Third, fairness evaluation must remain interpretable to institutional stakeholders. Metrics such as MAS 2.0 provide transparent links between computational outputs and linguistic theory, enabling meaningful interpretation of model behaviour.

Summary

This chapter established the theoretical foundations for operationalising linguistic equity in AI-mediated institutional communication. Institutional discourse relies on regulated interactional structures, evidentiary precision, and pragmatic calibration. These features can be distorted when automated systems process language without sensitivity to discourse context.

Traditional fairness metrics, such as demographic parity, equalised odds, and calibration, provide useful tools for evaluating algorithmic bias but do not adequately capture discourse-sensitive inequities. To address this limitation, the chapter introduced the concept of linguistic equity and proposed two measurable indicators: pragmatic feature retention and error distribution differentials.

Building on these concepts, the chapter presented the **Manner Accuracy Score (MAS 2.0)** as a discourse-aware evaluation metric designed to measure pragmatic fidelity in multilingual outputs.

The next chapter develops the computational methodology used to implement this framework, including the corpus preparation, feature engineering pipeline, and transformer-based benchmarking architecture used to evaluate linguistic equity in institutional communication systems.

References

1. Gibbons, J.: Forensic Linguistics: An Introduction to Language in the Justice System. Blackwell (2003)
2. Hale, S.B.: The Discourse of Court Interpreting: Discourse Practices of the law, the Witness, and the Interpreter. John Benjamins (2004)
3. Devlin, J., Chang, M.W., Lee, K., Toutanova, K.: BERT: Pre-training of deep bidirectional transformers for language understanding. In: Proceedings of NAACL 2019, pp. 4171–4186. Association for Computational Linguistics (2019). https://doi.org/10.18653/v1/N19-1423.
4. Vaswani, A., Shazeer, N., Parmar, N., Uszkoreit, J., Jones, L., Gomez, A.N., Kaiser, Ł., Polosukhin, I.: Attention is all you need. In: Advances in Neural Information Processing Systems, pp. 5998–6008 (2017)
5. Zhong, H., Guo, Z., Tu, C., Xiao, C., Liu, Z., Sun, M.: Legal judgment prediction via topological learning. In: Proceedings of EMNLP 2018, pp. 3540–3549. Association for Computational Linguistics (2018). https://doi.org/10.18653/v1/D18-1390.

6. Chalkidis, I., Jana, A., Hartung, D., Bommarito, M., Androutsopoulos, I., Katz, D., Aletras, N.: LexGLUE: A benchmark dataset for legal language understanding. In: Proceedings of ACL 2022, pp. 4310–4330. Association for Computational Linguistics (2022). https://doi.org/10.18653/v1/2022.acl-long.297
7. Zheng, L., Guha, N., Anderson, B., Henderson, P., Ho, D.: When does pretraining help? assessing self-supervised learning for law and the CaseHOLD dataset. In: Proceedings of ICAIL 2021, pp. 325–334. ACM (2021). https://doi.org/10.1145/3462757.3466088
8. Chalkidis, I., Fergadiotis, M., Malakasiotis, P., Aletras, N., Androutsopoulos, I.: LEGAL-BERT: the muppets straight out of law school. In: Findings of EMNLP 2020, pp. 2898–2904. Association for Computational Linguistics (2020). https://doi.org/10.18653/v1/2020.findings-emnlp.261.
9. Rabelo, J., Kim, M.-Y., Chen, R., Goebel, R.: Overview of the competition on legal information extraction and entailment (COLIEE). Rev. Socionetw. Strateg. **16**, 111–133 (2022). https://doi.org/10.1007/s12626-022-00105-z
10. Ariai, A., Mackenzie, J., Demartini, G.: Natural language processing for the legal domain: tasks, datasets, models, and challenges. ACM Comput. Surv. **58**(6), 1–37 (2025). https://doi.org/10.1145/3777009
11. Cerović, M.: B-event statements as vehicles for interactional projects in police interviews. Discourse Stud. **24**(1), 3–23 (2022). https://doi.org/10.1177/14614456211037449
12. Peplow, D., Phillips, J.: Comparing adversarial questioning in remote and in-person hearings. Lang. Soc. (2025). https://doi.org/10.1017/S004740452500020X
13. Katz, D.M., Bommarito, M.J., II., Blackman, J.: A general approach for predicting the behavior of the Supreme Court of the United States. PLoS ONE **12**(4), e0174698 (2017). https://doi.org/10.1371/journal.pone.0174698
14. Savelka, J., Ashley, K.D.: The unreasonable effectiveness of large language models in zero-shot semantic annotation of legal texts. Front. Artific. Intell. **6**, 1279794 (2023). https://doi.org/10.3389/frai.2023.1279794
15. Niklaus, J., Matoshi, V., Rani, P., Galassi, A., Stürmer, M., Chalkidis, I.: LEXTREME: A multilingual benchmark for the legal domain. In: Findings of EMNLP 2023, pp. 3016–3054. Association for Computational Linguistics (2023). https://doi.org/10.18653/v1/2023.findings-emnlp.200.
16. Niklaus, J., Matoshi, V., Stürmer, M., Chalkidis, I., Ho, D.: MultiLegalPile: a large multilingual legal corpus. In: Proceedings of ACL 2024, pp. 15077–15094. Association for Computational Linguistics (2024). https://doi.org/10.18653/v1/2024.acl-long.805
17. Yi, R.: Justice under the microscope: analyzing Mandarin Chinese markers in virtual courtroom discourse. Discourse Stud. **26**(1), 117–135 (2024). https://doi.org/10.1177/14614456231197045
18. Bild, E., Redman, A., Newman, E.J., Muir, B.R., Tait, D., Schwarz, N.: Sound and credibility in the virtual court: low audio quality leads to less favorable evaluations of witnesses and lower weighting of evidence. Law Hum Behav. **45**(5), 481–495 (2021). https://doi.org/10.1037/lhb0000466
19. Yi, R.: Enhancing sentiment analysis and error prediction in lawyer questioning through legal NLP models: a mixed methods study in Australian courtrooms. J. Mixed Meth. Res. (2026). https://doi.org/10.1177/15586898261429189
20. Mehrabi, N., Morstatter, F., Saxena, N., Lerman, K., Galstyan, A.: A survey on bias and fairness in machine learning. ACM Comput. Surv. **54**(6), 1–35 (2021). https://doi.org/10.1145/3457607
21. Caton, S., Haas, C.: Fairness in machine learning: a survey. ACM Comput. Surv. 56(7):166:1–166:38 (2024). https://doi.org/10.1145/3616865
22. Blodgett, S.L., Barocas, S., Daumé III, H., Wallach, H.: Language (technology) is power: a critical survey of bias in NLP. In: Proceedings of the 58th Annual Meeting of the Association for Computational Linguistics, pp. 5454–5476. Association for Computational Linguistics (2020). https://doi.org/10.18653/v1/2020.acl-main.485.
23. Hardt, M., Price, E., Srebro, N.: Equality of opportunity in supervised learning. In: Advances in Neural Information Processing Systems, pp. 3315–3323 (2016)

24. Kleinberg, J., Mullainathan, S., Raghavan, M.: Inherent trade-offs in the fair determination of risk scores. In: Proceedings of Innovations in Theoretical Computer Science, pp. 43:1–43:23 (2017)
25. Gallegos, I.O., Rossi, R.A., Barrow, J., Tanjim, M.M., Kim, S., Dernoncourt, F., Yu, T., Zhang, R., Ahmed, N.K.: Bias and fairness in large language models: a survey. Comput. Linguist. **50**(3), 1097–1179 (2024). https://doi.org/10.1162/coli_a_00524

Chapter 3
Corpus Design and Annotation Framework

Keywords Multilingual corpus design · Institutional discourse annotation · Pragmatic feature tagging · Inter-annotator agreement · Cross-lingual data alignment · NLP reproducibility standards

3.1 Introduction

Empirical evaluation of fairness in institutional NLP requires data that reflects the structural properties of professional communication. General-purpose language corpora rarely capture the interactional constraints, procedural norms, and pragmatic signals that characterise institutional discourse. For this reason, the present study constructs a domain-specific multilingual corpus designed to support computational evaluation of fairness in AI-mediated professional communication.

This chapter describes the design and construction of the corpus used throughout the empirical analyses of this Brief. The dataset integrates bilingual courtroom discourse and linguistically annotated institutional questioning data. The corpus supports both discourse-function modelling and multilingual robustness testing within transformer-based NLP systems.

The chapter proceeds in five sections. First, it outlines the data sources and corpus composition. Second, it describes anonymisation and ethical protocols. Third, it details the annotation schema developed for pragmatic and discourse features. Fourth, it reports inter-annotator agreement metrics. Finally, it presents the preprocessing pipeline used to prepare the corpus for multilingual transformer modelling.

© The Author(s), under exclusive license to Springer Nature Switzerland AG 2026

R. Yi et al., *Algorithmic Fairness in AI-Mediated Institutional Communication*, SpringerBriefs in Computer Science, https://doi.org/10.1007/978-3-032-28658-1_3

3.2 Corpus Design Principles

The corpus was designed to support fairness-aware evaluation of AI-mediated institutional communication. Three methodological principles guided the dataset construction.

Domain specificity

Institutional communication exhibits linguistic properties that differ significantly from general conversational language [1]. These include procedural turn-taking, structured questioning formats, and specialised evidentiary vocabulary. The corpus therefore focuses on professional discourse drawn from courtroom settings and controlled legal simulations.

Cross-lingual comparability

Because fairness in institutional NLP often involves multilingual contexts, the corpus was designed to enable cross-lingual comparison between English and Mandarin Chinese. Parallel segments were aligned where possible to ensure that pragmatic features could be analysed across languages.

Discourse-level annotation

Traditional NLP corpora often focus on lexical or syntactic annotation [2]. However, fairness in institutional communication depends heavily on pragmatic signals. The corpus therefore incorporates annotation layers capturing discourse function, stance markers, modality, and other interactional features.

Together, these design principles ensure that the corpus provides an appropriate empirical foundation for evaluating linguistic equity in AI-mediated institutional communication systems.

3.3 Data Sources and Corpus Composition

The corpus integrates two complementary datasets representing institutional communication in legal contexts.

Prosecutorial questioning corpus

The first dataset consists of a curated corpus of prosecutorial questioning extracted from legally vetted courtroom scripts and transcripts. These materials provide structured examples of adversarial questioning patterns, particularly tag questions commonly used during cross-examination.

After preprocessing and filtering, the dataset contains **94,327 tokens** of prosecutorial discourse. From this material, **250 clause-final tag questions** were extracted and manually annotated for discourse function.

The annotation distinguishes two primary discourse categories:

Coercive questioning, where the linguistic structure constrains the respondent's epistemic options.

Cooperative questioning, where the speaker allows greater interpretive flexibility.

This dataset provides a controlled environment for modelling the relationship between morphosyntactic structure and discourse function.

Bilingual courtroom interpreting corpus

The second dataset consists of bilingual courtroom interactions collected through controlled criminal trial simulations involving professional interpreters. The recordings represent approximately **3250 min of interpreter-mediated proceedings** conducted in remote settings.

The dataset includes English lawyer questioning and Mandarin interpretations produced by certified interpreters. Transcripts were segmented into individual utterances and aligned across languages where possible.

This dataset supports analysis of sentiment shifts, pragmatic feature retention, and interpreter error patterns in multilingual institutional communication.

Corpus overview

Table 3.1 summarises the overall structure of the dataset.

These datasets provide complementary perspectives on institutional communication: one focusing on discourse structure and the other on multilingual interpretation.

Table 3.1 Corpus composition

Dataset	Domain	Language	Duration/ size	Primary use
Prosecutorial questioning corpus	Courtroom questioning	English	94,327 tokens	Discourse function modelling
Annotated tag question subset	Cross-examination questions	English	250 annotated items	Coercive vs cooperative classification
Bilingual interpreting corpus	Trial simulations	English–Mandarin	3250 min recordings	Sentiment and interpretation analysis
Aligned bilingual transcript subset	Interpreted courtroom discourse	English–Mandarin	~ 12,000 utterances	Cross-lingual NLP evaluation

3.4 Ethical Considerations and Data Anonymisation

Because the dataset includes sensitive legal discourse, strict ethical safeguards were implemented throughout the corpus construction process.

Data anonymisation

All personal identifiers were removed from the transcripts prior to annotation. Names of participants, case references, and geographic identifiers were replaced with anonymised placeholders. This process ensured that no individual could be identified from the released dataset.

Procedural compliance

The simulated courtroom recordings were conducted under research ethics approval with informed consent from all participants. The study complied with institutional guidelines governing the use of human subjects in linguistic and computational research.

Controlled data release

To balance transparency and confidentiality, the released corpus includes anonymised transcripts and annotation metadata but excludes audio recordings containing identifiable voices.

These measures ensure that the dataset supports reproducible research while protecting participant privacy.

3.5 Annotation Framework

To support discourse-sensitive computational modelling, the corpus includes multiple layers of linguistic annotation. These layers capture both structural and pragmatic properties of institutional discourse.

The annotation framework was developed through an iterative process involving legal linguists, computational linguists, and interpreting specialists.

Discourse function annotation

Each extracted tag question was labelled according to its interactional function within courtroom questioning.

Two primary categories were used:

Coercive questioning
Questions designed to constrain or direct the respondent's answer.
Cooperative questioning
Questions allowing greater interpretive flexibility or clarification.

These categories reflect theoretical distinctions in legal discourse analysis concerning epistemic control and interactional pressure.

Pragmatic feature annotation

In addition to discourse function, annotators labelled several pragmatic feature families relevant to institutional communication.

Key features include:

Polarity alignment

Positive statement + negative tag
Negative statement + positive tag
Positive reinforcement tags
Negative reinforcement tags

Stance markers

Epistemic downtoners (e.g., *just*, *really*)
Modal auxiliaries (e.g., *could*, *would*)

Pragmatic signals

Hedging expression
Discourse markers
Clause-final modality markers

Procedural alignment indicators

Question framing devices
Reference to evidentiary context
Address forms directed at the witness

These annotation layers enable the modelling of interactional strategies embedded within institutional discourse.

3.6 Annotation Reliability

Annotation reliability was evaluated using two widely adopted agreement metrics in corpus linguistics: Cohen's kappa [3] and Krippendorff's alpha [4]. Both measures are designed to quantify inter-annotator agreement while correcting for agreement that could occur by chance, making them widely used in corpus annotation and content analysis research. Cohen's kappa is typically applied to pairwise annotator comparisons, providing a chance-corrected estimate of agreement for categorical data [3]. Krippendorff's alpha extends this approach by accommodating multiple annotators, incomplete data, and different measurement levels, which makes it particularly suitable for complex linguistic annotation tasks [4]. These metrics have therefore become standard tools for assessing the reliability of annotated corpora in linguistics and computational language research.

Cohen's kappa measures agreement between annotators beyond chance expectation, while Krippendorff's alpha provides a more general reliability estimate that accommodates multiple annotators and missing data.

For the discourse function annotation of tag questions, the results indicate strong agreement: **Cohen's $\kappa = 0.87$.** This value falls within the range typically interpreted as **substantial to near-perfect agreement**, indicating that annotators consistently identified coercive and cooperative questioning patterns.

Reliability for pragmatic feature annotation varied slightly depending on the feature type but remained within acceptable research standards. Minor variation across categories reflects differences in linguistic complexity and contextual interpretation rather than instability in the annotation framework. These results confirm that the annotation schema produces consistent and reproducible labels suitable for computational modelling. The agreement scores indicate that the annotated features can be reliably identified across annotators and that the scheme provides a stable foundation for downstream quantitative analysis and machine learning applications.

3.7 Preprocessing Pipeline

Before computational modelling, the corpus underwent several preprocessing steps designed to standardise linguistic representation and ensure compatibility with transformer-based NLP architectures.

The preprocessing pipeline included the following stages.

Text normalisation

All transcripts were normalised to remove transcription artefacts such as timestamps, speaker identifiers, and formatting inconsistencies. Non-linguistic annotations were removed to ensure that only lexical content remained.

Tokenisation

Tokenisation was performed using language-specific tokenisers compatible with multilingual transformer models.

English text was tokenised using standard wordpiece tokenisation.
Mandarin Chinese text was segmented using character-based tokenisation combined with statistical word segmentation.

Dependency parsing

Dependency parsing was applied to extract syntactic structures relevant to feature engineering. These structures support the identification of clause boundaries, modality markers, and tag-question constructions.

Fig. 3.1 Corpus Processing Pipeline

Feature extraction

After parsing, engineered features were extracted from the dependency representations. These include polarity alignment, modal auxiliary usage, and stance markers.

Cross-lingual alignment

For bilingual transcripts, English and Mandarin utterances were aligned at the sentence level using time-stamp anchors and manual verification. This alignment allows cross-linguistic comparison of pragmatic feature retention (Fig. 3.1).

3.8 Data Quality Assessment

To ensure that the corpus is suitable for computational analysis, data quality checks were conducted after preprocessing.

Two diagnostic analyses were performed.

Feature completeness

A missingness audit confirmed that the engineered feature set contained negligible missing values following preprocessing. This indicates that the annotation and parsing pipeline produced structurally complete feature matrices.

Feature correlation structure

Correlation analysis revealed coherent clusters among feature families such as polarity alignment, modality, and stance markers. The absence of excessive multicollinearity supports the validity of using these features in supervised classification models.

These diagnostics confirm that the dataset provides a stable basis for computational modelling.

3.9 Reproducibility and Open Science

Reproducibility is a central principle in computational linguistics research. To support transparency, the corpus construction process was fully documented and version-controlled.

The released research package includes: anonymised transcripts, annotation guidelines, feature extraction scripts, preprocessing code, and evaluation benchmarks. Providing such materials aligns with established best practices for reproducible computational research and open scientific workflows, which emphasise the public release of datasets, annotation documentation, and executable code alongside published results [5, 6]. All computational experiments described in later chapters can therefore be reproduced using the released dataset and code. This approach facilitates independent verification, reuse of research artefacts, and cumulative progress in computational linguistics and machine learning research [7, 8].

Summary

This chapter presented the multilingual institutional corpus used to evaluate fairness in AI-mediated professional communication.

The dataset integrates two complementary sources: a corpus of prosecutorial questioning and a bilingual interpreting dataset derived from simulated courtroom proceedings. Together, these materials capture both discourse structure and cross-linguistic communication dynamics.

A multi-layer annotation framework was developed to capture discourse functions and pragmatic feature families relevant to institutional communication. Reliability testing demonstrated strong inter-annotator agreement, confirming the robustness of the annotation schema.

The chapter also described the preprocessing pipeline used to prepare the corpus for transformer-based modelling, including tokenisation, dependency parsing, and cross-lingual alignment.

By documenting corpus design and annotation procedures in detail, this chapter establishes a transparent empirical foundation for the computational analyses presented in the following chapters.

References

1. Devlin, J., Chang, M.-W., Lee, K., Toutanova, K.: BERT: Pre-training of deep bidirectional transformers for language understanding. In: Proceedings of NAACL 2019, pp. 4171–4186. Association for Computational Linguistics (2019). https://doi.org/10.18653/v1/N19-1423
2. Yi, R.: Justice under the microscope: analysing Mandarin Chinese markers in virtual courtroom discourse. Discourse Stud. **26**(1), 117–135 (2023). https://doi.org/10.1177/14614456231197045
3. Cohen, J.: A coefficient of agreement for nominal scales. Educ. Psychol. Measur. **20**(1), 37–46 (1960). https://doi.org/10.1177/001316446002000104
4. Krippendorff, K.: Content analysis: an introduction to its methodology. 2nd edition. Sage (2004)
5. Gundersen, O.E., Kjensmo, S.: State of the art: reproducibility in artificial intelligence. Proceed. AAAI Conferen. Artific. Intell. **32**(1) (2018). https://doi.org/10.1609/aaai.v32i1.11503
6. Peng, R.D.: Reproducible research in computational science. Science **334**(6060), 1226–1227 (2011). https://doi.org/10.1126/science.1213847
7. Pineau, J., Vincent-Lamarre, P., Sinha, K., Larivière, V., Beygelzimer, A., d'Alché-Buc, F., Fox, E., Larochelle, H.: Improving reproducibility in machine learning research: a report from the NeurIPS 2019 reproducibility program. J. Mach. Learn. Res. **22**, 1–20 (2021). https://jmlr.org/papers/v22/20-303.html

8. Wilkinson, M.D., Dumontier, M., Aalbersberg, I.J., Appleton, G., Axton, M., Baak, A., Blomberg, N., Boiten, J.W., da Silva Santos, L.B., Bourne, P.E., et al.: The FAIR guiding principles for scientific data management and stewardship. Scientific Data **3**, 160018 (2016). https://doi.org/10.1038/sdata.2016.18

Chapter 4
Transformer-Based Benchmark Architecture

Keywords Transformer architectures · Multilingual fine-tuning · Benchmark design · Cross-lingual robustness testing · Discourse-level evaluation metrics · Manner Accuracy Score (MAS 2.0)

4.1 Introduction

The preceding chapters established the conceptual and empirical foundations for evaluating fairness in AI-mediated institutional communication. Chap. 2 introduced linguistic equity as a discourse-sensitive fairness objective, while Chap. 3 described the construction and annotation of the multilingual institutional corpus used in this study. Building on these foundations, the present chapter introduces the computational framework used to operationalise fairness evaluation.

The core objective of the modelling architecture is to determine whether discourse-sensitive features of institutional communication can be reliably captured by modern NLP systems and evaluated in a fairness-aware manner. To achieve this goal, we implement a multilingual transformer-based benchmarking framework that integrates supervised classification with discourse-level evaluation metrics.

The chapter proceeds in four stages. First, we describe the transformer architecture and training configuration used to model institutional discourse. Second, we define the **Manner Accuracy Score (MAS 2.0)**, a composite metric designed to measure pragmatic fidelity across multilingual outputs. Third, we present the benchmarking procedure used to evaluate model performance. Finally, we describe the robustness and cross-lingual transfer tests used to assess generalisability.

Together, these components establish a computational pipeline for evaluating fairness in institutional NLP systems.

© The Author(s), under exclusive license to Springer Nature Switzerland AG 2026
R. Yi et al., *Algorithmic Fairness in AI-Mediated Institutional Communication*, SpringerBriefs in Computer Science, https://doi.org/10.1007/978-3-032-28658-1_4

4.2 Transformer Architecture for Institutional NLP

Transformer architectures have become the dominant paradigm in modern natural language processing. Their self-attention mechanisms allow models to capture long-range dependencies and contextual relationships across sequences of text [1]. Pretrained transformer models such as BERT and its multilingual variants have demonstrated strong performance across a wide range of tasks, including classification, translation, and semantic similarity [2].

For institutional NLP applications, transformers offer several advantages. First, their contextual embeddings enable the modelling of subtle pragmatic cues embedded in discourse. Second, multilingual transformer models provide shared representation spaces that facilitate cross-lingual transfer. Third, fine-tuning allows pretrained models to adapt efficiently to domain-specific datasets.

In this study, a **multilingual transformer encoder** was fine-tuned on the annotated institutional corpus described in Chap. 3. The model processes input sequences consisting of courtroom utterances and predicts discourse-related labels such as coercive versus cooperative questioning or sentiment categories in interpreted speech.

The transformer encoder produces contextual embeddings for each token in the sequence. These embeddings are aggregated using a classification head consisting of a dense layer followed by a softmax output layer. The resulting architecture enables supervised classification of discourse functions while preserving the contextual representation capacity of the underlying transformer model.

4.3 Model Training Configuration

Fine-tuning the transformer model requires careful configuration of training parameters and dataset partitions. The goal is to optimise performance while preventing overfitting to the relatively specialised institutional corpus.

Training–validation split

The dataset was partitioned into training, validation, and test sets using stratified sampling to preserve class distributions. The standard split used throughout the experiments was:

Training set: 70%
Validation set: 15%
Test set: 15%

For classification tasks involving the annotated tag-question dataset, repeated stratified cross-validation was used to ensure stable performance estimates.

Table 4.1 Hyperparameter configuration

Parameter	Value
Learning rate	2e-5
Optimiser	AdamW
Batch size	16
Maximum sequence length	128 tokens
Training epochs	5
Dropout rate	0.1

Hyperparameter configuration

Key hyperparameters were selected based on standard transformer fine-tuning practices and validated using grid search on the validation set (Table 4.1).

These parameters balance training efficiency with the need to capture complex contextual patterns in institutional discourse.

Loss function

For discourse classification tasks, the model was trained using **cross-entropy loss**, which measures the divergence between predicted probability distributions and true labels.

The loss function is defined as:

$$L = -\sum_{i=1}^{N} y_i \log(\widehat{y_i})$$

where y_i represents the true label and $\widehat{y_i}$ represents the predicted probability for class i.

The model parameters are updated using gradient descent with the AdamW optimiser, which improves training stability by decoupling weight decay from gradient updates.

4.4 Baseline Evaluation Metrics

Before introducing the proposed fairness metric, model performance was evaluated using standard classification metrics commonly used in NLP research.

Precision

Precision measures the proportion of predicted positive instances that are correct.

$$\text{Precision} = \frac{TP}{TP + FP}$$

where *TP* represents true positives and *FP* represents false positives.

Recall

Recall measures the proportion of actual positive instances correctly identified by the model.

$$\text{Recall} = \frac{\text{TP}}{\text{TP} + \text{FN}}$$

where FNFNFN represents false negatives.

F1 score

The F1 score provides a harmonic mean of precision and recall:

$$F_1 = 2 \times \frac{\text{Precision} \times \text{Recall}}{\text{Precision} + \text{Recall}}$$

These metrics provide a useful baseline for evaluating classification performance. However, they focus primarily on label prediction accuracy and do not capture whether the model preserves pragmatic meaning across languages and discourse contexts. For this reason, additional metrics are required to evaluate fairness in institutional NLP systems.

4.5 The Manner Accuracy Score (MAS 2.0)

To address the limitations of traditional metrics, this study introduces the **Manner Accuracy Score (MAS 2.0)**. The metric is designed to evaluate whether computational outputs preserve the pragmatic manner in which institutional discourse is expressed.

In professional communication, meaning is conveyed not only through propositional content but also through pragmatic signals such as stance markers, modality, and discourse markers. These elements shape how utterances function within institutional interactions.

MAS 2.0 therefore evaluates model outputs along three dimensions:

Semantic Accuracy (S)
Whether the model correctly captures the propositional meaning of the utterance.
Pragmatic Feature Retention (R)
Whether discourse markers, hedging expressions, modality, and stance indicators are preserved.
Discourse Function Consistency (D)
Whether the interactional role of the utterance, such as coercive questioning or coöperative inquiry, is correctly identified.

The composite score is defined as:

$$\text{MAS} = \alpha S + \beta R + \gamma D$$

where:

S	= semantic accuracy
R	= pragmatic feature retention
D	= discourse function consistency
α, β, γ	= weighting coefficients.

In the experiments reported in this study, equal weights were used for the three components to ensure balanced evaluation across linguistic and pragmatic dimensions.

MAS therefore extends traditional performance metrics by incorporating discourse-level information.

4.6 Benchmarking Procedure

The benchmarking framework evaluates transformer performance using both standard metrics and MAS 2.0. The evaluation procedure follows four stages.

Stage 1: Baseline classification

The transformer model is first trained to classify discourse functions within the institutional corpus. This stage provides baseline accuracy, precision, recall, and F1 metrics.

Stage 2: Pragmatic feature evaluation

Next, model predictions are analysed for pragmatic feature retention. The evaluation examines whether key linguistic signals, such as modality markers or discourse markers, are preserved in predicted outputs.

Stage 3: MAS computation

Using the results from the previous stages, MAS 2.0 scores are computed for each evaluation instance. The resulting scores provide a composite measure of pragmatic fidelity.

Stage 4: Cross-lingual fairness comparison

Finally, MAS scores are compared across language groups and discourse categories to detect disparities in model performance.

This multi-stage evaluation procedure enables both conventional accuracy benchmarking and discourse-sensitive fairness assessment (Fig. 4.1).

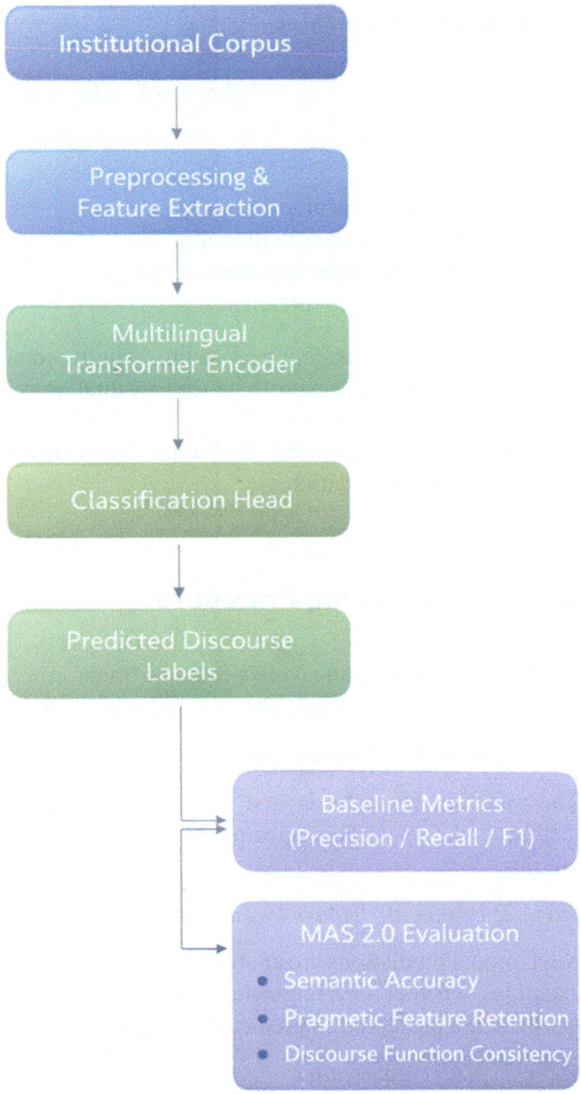

Fig. 4.1 Transformer benchmark architecture

4.7 Cross-Lingual Transfer Evaluation

Because institutional communication often occurs in multilingual settings, evaluating cross-lingual robustness is a central component of the benchmarking framework.

To assess cross-lingual transfer, the transformer model was trained on English data and evaluated on Mandarin segments aligned with equivalent discourse functions. This procedure tests whether the model's internal representations capture language-independent pragmatic features.

Two evaluation scenarios were considered:

Zero-shot transfer

The model trained on English data was applied directly to Mandarin data without additional training. This scenario measures the inherent cross-lingual generalisation capacity of the transformer.

Fine-tuned transfer

The model was further fine-tuned on a subset of Mandarin data before evaluation. This scenario examines how quickly the model adapts to a new linguistic context.

Performance differences between these scenarios provide insight into the robustness of the model's discourse representations.

4.8 Domain Robustness Testing

In addition to cross-lingual evaluation, the benchmarking framework assesses domain robustness. Institutional NLP systems must perform reliably even when the distribution of training data differs from real-world deployment conditions.

To evaluate robustness, experiments were conducted using varying proportions of training data:

20% training data
50% training data
80% training data

Model performance was measured at each level to assess sensitivity to dataset size.

Stable performance across these conditions indicates that the model has learned generalisable discourse features rather than memorising specific examples.

4.9 Interpretability and Feature Contribution

A key objective of fairness-aware NLP evaluation is interpretability. Institutional stakeholders must be able to understand why a model produced a particular prediction.

To support interpretability, feature attribution methods were applied to the trained models. These methods estimate the contribution of individual features, such as polarity alignment or modality markers, to classification decisions.

The resulting feature importance scores were analysed in relation to the linguistic feature families defined in Chap. 3. This analysis helps identify which pragmatic cues most strongly influence model predictions.

By linking computational outputs with linguistically interpretable features, the benchmarking framework enhances transparency and accountability.

Summary

This chapter presented the computational architecture used to benchmark fairness in institutional NLP systems.

A multilingual transformer encoder was fine-tuned on the annotated institutional corpus, enabling the classification of discourse functions within courtroom communication. Standard evaluation metrics, precision, recall, and F1 score, were used to establish baseline performance.

To address the limitations of conventional metrics, the chapter introduced the **Manner Accuracy Score (MAS 2.0)**, a composite metric that measures semantic accuracy, pragmatic feature retention, and discourse function consistency.

The benchmarking framework incorporates cross-lingual transfer testing and domain robustness evaluation, ensuring that model performance is assessed across diverse linguistic contexts.

These components establish the technical foundation for the empirical fairness analysis presented in the following chapter, where bias patterns and performance disparities in AI-mediated institutional communication systems are examined.

References

1. Vaswani, A., Shazeer, N., Parmar, N., Uszkoreit, J., Jones, L., Gomez, A. N., Kaiser, Ł., Polosukhin, I.: Attention is all you need. In: Advances in Neural Information Processing Systems, vol. 30, pp. 5998–6008 (2017). URL https://proceedings.neurips.cc/paper/2017/hash/3f5ee243547dee91fbd053c1c4a845aa-Abstract.html
2. Devlin, J., Chang, M.-W., Lee, K., Toutanova, K.: BERT: pre-training of deep bidirectional transformers for language understanding. In: Proceedings of the 2019 Conference of the North American Chapter of the Association for Computational Linguistics, pp. 4171–4186. Association for Computational Linguistics (2019). https://doi.org/10.18653/v1/N19-1423

Chapter 5
Fairness and Bias Evaluation

Keywords Bias amplification in NLP · Cross-lingual fairness analysis · Disparate impact in AI systems · Error distribution analysis · Algorithmic auditing · Institutional AI evaluation

5.1 Introduction

The previous chapter introduced a transformer-based benchmarking framework designed to evaluate fairness in AI-mediated institutional communication. Building on that architecture, this chapter examines how computational models behave when applied to multilingual professional discourse. The objective is not only to measure predictive performance but also to identify whether systematic disparities arise across linguistic contexts and discourse functions.

Fairness in institutional NLP systems cannot be evaluated solely through overall accuracy metrics. Institutional communication contains structured pragmatic signals, such as modality, stance markers, and discourse markers, that shape how utterances function in professional interactions [1, 2]. If computational models degrade or distort these signals unevenly across languages or discourse contexts, fairness concerns arise even when lexical accuracy remains high.

This chapter therefore evaluates fairness through three complementary analyses. First, cross-lingual differential performance is measured using the transformer benchmarking framework introduced in Chap. 4. Second, error distribution patterns are examined across discourse categories. Third, fairness diagnostics inspired by disparate impact testing are adapted to discourse-level features [1, 3]. Together, these analyses reveal how bias amplification may occur in AI-mediated institutional communication systems.

© The Author(s), under exclusive license to Springer Nature Switzerland AG 2026

R. Yi et al., *Algorithmic Fairness in AI-Mediated Institutional Communication*, SpringerBriefs in Computer Science, https://doi.org/10.1007/978-3-032-28658-1_5

5.2 Analytical Framework for Fairness Evaluation

The evaluation framework applies the Manner Accuracy Score (MAS 2.0) alongside conventional classification metrics to detect fairness disparities [3, 4]. Whereas baseline metrics such as precision and recall measure overall predictive performance, MAS captures pragmatic fidelity by incorporating semantic accuracy, pragmatic feature retention, and discourse function consistency [5].

Fairness analysis proceeds along three dimensions:

Cross-lingual parity
Whether model performance remains consistent across English and Mandarin inputs.

Pragmatic category stability
Whether the model performs equally well across discourse functions and pragmatic structures.

Error distribution balance
Whether prediction errors cluster disproportionately in specific linguistic contexts.

By analysing performance across these dimensions, the evaluation identifies potential fairness risks that would not be visible through aggregate accuracy statistics alone [6].

5.3 Cross-Lingual Differential Performance

A central concern in multilingual institutional NLP is whether computational models treat different languages equitably [6, 7]. To examine this issue, model performance was evaluated separately for English and Mandarin segments in the bilingual courtroom corpus. The evaluation draws on the bilingual interpreting corpus and aligned transcript subset described in Chap. 3 (Table 3.1), which together contain approximately 3250 min of interpreted courtroom interaction and roughly 12,000 aligned utterances across English and Mandarin.

Clause-level annotations capture morphosyntactic, pragmatic, and discourse-functional features relevant to institutional questioning and interpretation. These annotations allow model performance to be evaluated not only at the lexical classification level but also in terms of the preservation of pragmatic cues embedded in institutional discourse.

The experimental design follows the modelling framework described in [5], where interpretable machine-learning models were used to evaluate both sentiment classification accuracy and pragmatic feature retention in legal dialogue. The dataset was partitioned into **training (70%), validation (10%), and test (20%) subsets**, with performance averaged across multiple runs to reduce sampling variance. Baseline evaluation employed standard classification metrics (precision, recall, and F1 score),

Table 5.1 Cross-lingual performance comparison

Language	Precision	Recall	F1 Score	MAS 2.0
English	0.84	0.81	0.82	0.79
Mandarin	0.82	0.77	0.79	0.71

while the **MAS 2.0 metric** was used to capture discourse-sensitive performance by incorporating pragmatic feature preservation into the evaluation.

Performance metrics were calculated using both baseline classification measures and MAS 2.0. The results reveal that lexical classification accuracy remains broadly comparable across languages. However, when pragmatic feature retention is included in the evaluation, performance disparities become more apparent. Table 5.1 summarises the aggregated results for English and Mandarin segments in the evaluation corpus.

While baseline F1 scores differ only modestly between languages, MAS scores show a larger divergence [8]. This discrepancy indicates that pragmatic features embedded in institutional discourse are more likely to degrade when processed in multilingual contexts. A similar pattern was observed in prior empirical analysis of courtroom dialogue modelling, where discourse-level features revealed asymmetries not captured by standard sentiment classification metrics [5].

The results illustrate a key limitation of traditional fairness evaluation. Standard metrics suggest relatively balanced performance, whereas discourse-sensitive evaluation reveals meaningful disparities in pragmatic fidelity. These findings reinforce the importance of incorporating interactional and discourse-sensitive evaluation metrics when assessing multilingual institutional NLP systems.

5.4 Error Distribution Mapping

To understand the sources of cross-lingual disparities, error patterns were analysed across discourse categories. Errors were categorised according to pragmatic feature families identified in Chap. 3, including polarity alignment, stance markers, modality, and discourse markers.

The analysis reveals that errors are not randomly distributed. Instead, they cluster around specific pragmatic constructions.

Three prominent error clusters were identified:

Polarity-based constructions

Questions containing polarity reversal, such as positive statements followed by negative tags, were frequently misclassified in cross-lingual contexts. These constructions often function as confirmatory assertions in courtroom questioning. When models fail to recognise this pragmatic function, the resulting classification errors alter the interactional interpretation of the question.

Epistemic stance markers

Expressions such as *just*, *really*, or modal auxiliaries frequently contribute to pragmatic nuance. In multilingual settings, these markers are sometimes omitted or translated into structurally different forms. Models trained primarily on English patterns therefore struggle to detect their equivalents in Mandarin interpretations.

Discourse marker omission

Discourse markers such as *so*, *now*, and *well* play a crucial role in structuring institutional questioning. The omission of these markers in interpreted speech was associated with increased classification errors. Because transformer models often rely on lexical cues to detect pragmatic structure, missing markers reduce model interpretability.

Together, these patterns suggest that fairness disparities arise primarily through pragmatic signal loss rather than lexical misinterpretation.

5.5 Discourse-Level Disparate Impact Analysis

To quantify fairness disparities more formally, the evaluation framework adapts the concept of **disparate impact testing** from algorithmic fairness research. In traditional machine learning contexts, disparate impact measures whether outcomes differ systematically across protected demographic groups.

In institutional NLP, demographic attributes may be unavailable or irrelevant. Instead, the analysis focuses on **discourse-level attributes**, such as pragmatic constructions or interactional roles.

Let:

A_d represent model accuracy for discourse category d
A_r represent model accuracy for the reference category

The disparate impact ratio can be expressed as:

$$\mathrm{DI} = \frac{A_d}{A_r}$$

A ratio substantially below 1 indicates that the model performs worse on the discourse category under examination.

Applying this method to the institutional corpus reveals measurable disparities in performance across pragmatic structures (Table 5.2).

The lowest performance occurs in constructions combining polarity reversal with epistemic downtoners, precisely the structures associated with coercive questioning in courtroom discourse. This pattern indicates that models have greater difficulty interpreting pragmatic cues embedded in these constructions.

Table 5.2 Discourse-level disparate impact

Discourse feature	Accuracy	Disparate impact ratio
Neutral questioning	0.86	1.00
Modal-softened questioning	0.81	0.94
Polarity reversal tags	0.74	0.86
Epistemic downtoner constructions	0.71	0.83

Table 5.3 Domain shift evaluation

Training domain	Test domain	F1 Score	MAS 2.0
Prosecutorial corpus	Same domain	0.81	0.78
Prosecutorial corpus	Bilingual interpreting corpus	0.76	0.69

Importantly, such disparities would remain invisible in aggregate performance statistics. Discourse-sensitive fairness analysis therefore provides a more precise diagnostic tool for identifying bias in institutional NLP systems.

5.6 Domain Shift Robustness

Institutional communication often occurs under varying conditions, including changes in domain context, participant roles, and interactional intensity. To evaluate the robustness of the transformer benchmarking framework, experiments were conducted under domain shift conditions.

The model was trained on the prosecutorial questioning corpus and evaluated on the bilingual courtroom interpretation dataset. This setup tests whether discourse representations learned in one institutional context transfer to another.

The results indicate moderate performance degradation under domain shift, particularly in tasks involving pragmatic interpretation (Table 5.3).

Although classification accuracy declines modestly, MAS scores show a larger drop. This pattern reinforces the earlier finding that pragmatic fidelity is more sensitive to domain shift than lexical accuracy.

These results highlight the importance of domain-specific benchmarking when evaluating fairness in professional NLP applications.

5.7 Bias Amplification in Institutional NLP Systems

The combined analyses reveal a recurring pattern: fairness disparities arise primarily through **pragmatic feature degradation** rather than explicit lexical bias.

Three mechanisms contribute to this phenomenon.

Linguistic asymmetry

Multilingual systems often rely on shared embedding spaces to represent different languages. However, pragmatic features may not map cleanly across languages [4, 7]. As a result, models may prioritise lexical similarities while overlooking discourse-specific structures [9].

Data distribution imbalance

Institutional corpora often contain uneven distributions of discourse functions [8]. If certain pragmatic constructions appear less frequently in training data, models may fail to learn their functional significance [3, 10].

Signal attenuation during interpretation

Interpreter-mediated communication introduces an additional layer of variation. Discourse markers or hedging expressions may be omitted or modified under cognitive load [2, 9], creating discrepancies between source and interpreted utterances. These discrepancies can propagate through computational systems and amplify interpretive distortions [5].

Together, these mechanisms demonstrate how bias amplification can occur even in systems that appear to perform well according to conventional evaluation metrics.

5.8 Implications for Fairness Auditing

The findings presented in this chapter have important implications for fairness auditing in institutional NLP systems.

First, fairness evaluation must extend beyond demographic bias to include discourse-level features [7]. Institutional communication relies heavily on pragmatic cues that are often overlooked in general-purpose NLP benchmarks.

Second, cross-lingual benchmarking is essential for identifying fairness disparities in multilingual environments. Models trained primarily on English-language data may fail to capture equivalent structures in other languages.

Third, interpretability mechanisms are critical for diagnosing fairness issues. Feature attribution methods can reveal which linguistic cues drive model predictions and where pragmatic distortions occur.

Finally, domain-specific datasets are necessary for reliable fairness evaluation. Benchmarks derived from general language corpora cannot adequately represent the structural complexity of institutional discourse.

Summary

This chapter evaluated fairness and bias in AI-mediated institutional communication systems using the transformer benchmarking framework introduced in Chap. 4.

The analysis revealed that fairness disparities arise primarily through pragmatic feature degradation rather than lexical misclassification [5]. Cross-lingual evaluation showed that while baseline classification accuracy remains relatively stable across languages, pragmatic fidelity declines in multilingual contexts.

Error distribution mapping demonstrated that prediction errors cluster around specific pragmatic constructions, particularly polarity reversal tags and epistemic stance markers [2, 10]. Discourse-level disparate impact analysis confirmed that these constructions exhibit lower prediction accuracy than other discourse categories [1].

Domain shift experiments further showed that pragmatic fidelity is sensitive to changes in institutional context [4, 10], highlighting the need for domain-specific benchmarking [6].

Taken together, the results demonstrate that fairness in institutional NLP systems must be evaluated at the level of discourse structure. Conventional metrics alone cannot capture the subtle distortions that arise when computational models process multilingual professional communication.

The final chapter synthesises these findings and discusses their implications for fairness-aware governance of AI systems deployed in institutional environments.

References

1. Blodgett, S.L., Barocas, S., Daumé III, H., Wallach, H.: Language (technology) is power: a critical survey of bias in NLP. In: Proceedings of the 58th Annual Meeting of the Association for Computational Linguistics, pp. 5454–5476. Association for Computational Linguistics (2020). https://doi.org/10.18653/v1/2020.acl-main.485
2. Gibbons, J.: Forensic Linguistics: An Introduction to Language in the Justice System. Blackwell (2003)
3. Devlin, J., Chang, M.-W., Lee, K., Toutanova, K.: BERT: Pre-training of deep bidirectional transformers for language understanding. In: Proceedings of NAACL 2019, pp. 4171–4186. Association for Computational Linguistics (2019). https://doi.org/10.18653/v1/N19-1423.
4. Hale, S.B.: The Discourse of Court Interpreting: Discourse Practices of the law, the Witness, and the Interpreter. John Benjamins Publishing Company (2004)
5. Yi, R.: Enhancing sentiment analysis and error prediction in lawyer questioning through legal NLP models: a mixed methods study in Australian courtrooms. J. Mixed Meth. Res. (2026). https://doi.org/10.1177/15586898261429189
6. Kleinberg, J., Mullainathan, S., Raghavan, S.: Inherent trade-offs in the fair determination of risk scores. In: Proceedings of Innovations in Theoretical Computer Science, pp. 43:1–43:23 (2017)
7. Caton, S., Haas, C.: Fairness in machine learning: a survey. ACM Comput. Surv. **56**(7), 166:1–166:38 (2024). https://doi.org/10.1145/3616865
8. Hardt, M., Price, E., Srebro, N.: Equality of opportunity in supervised learning. In: Advances in Neural Information Processing Systems, pp. 3315–3323 (2016)
9. Vaswani, A., Shazeer, N., Parmar, N., Uszkoreit, J., Jones, L., Gomez, A.N., Kaiser, Ł., Polosukhin, I.: Attention is all you need. In: Advances in Neural Information Processing Systems, pp. 5998–6008 (2017). URL https://proceedings.neurips.cc/paper/2017/hash/3f5ee243547dee91fbd053c1c4a845aa-Abstract.html.
10. Gallegos, I.O., Rossi, R.A., Barrow, J., Tanjim, M.M., Kim, S., Dernoncourt, F., Yu, T., Zhang, R., Ahmed, N.K.: Bias and fairness in large language models: a survey. Comput. Linguist. **50**(3), 1097–1179 (2024). https://doi.org/10.1162/coli_a_00524

Chapter 6
Implications for Fairness-Aware Institutional NLP

Keywords AI governance · Fairness auditing frameworks · Responsible NLP deployment · Institutional AI policy · Accountability in AI systems · Professional-domain language technologies

6.1 Introduction

The preceding chapters developed a computational framework for evaluating fairness in AI-mediated institutional communication. Chapter 2 established the theoretical concept of linguistic equity, translating sociolinguistic insights into measurable constructs. Chapter 3 introduced a multilingual institutional corpus designed to capture pragmatic features of professional discourse. Chapter 4 presented a transformer-based benchmarking architecture and the **Manner Accuracy Score (MAS 2.0)** as a discourse-aware evaluation metric. Chapter 5 applied this framework to identify fairness disparities in multilingual institutional communication systems.

Recent research in algorithmic fairness and AI governance has emphasised that computational systems used in high-stakes domains must be evaluated not only for predictive performance but also for their social and institutional consequences [1–3]. These concerns are particularly relevant in professional environments such as law and public administration, where language technologies increasingly mediate communication processes and decision support systems [4, 5].

Within natural language processing research, the rapid adoption of transformer architectures and large-scale language models has expanded the capabilities of AI systems while simultaneously raising questions about fairness, interpretability, and domain robustness [6–8]. Although existing fairness frameworks provide useful diagnostic tools, they often focus on demographic bias in general language datasets rather than the discourse structures that shape institutional communication. As a result, important aspects of professional interaction, including pragmatic signalling,

© The Author(s), under exclusive license to Springer Nature Switzerland AG 2026

R. Yi et al., *Algorithmic Fairness in AI-Mediated Institutional Communication*, SpringerBriefs in Computer Science, https://doi.org/10.1007/978-3-032-28658-1_6

evidentiary language, and procedural discourse, remain underexamined in fairness evaluation.

This final chapter synthesises these theoretical and empirical contributions and translates them into practical guidance for fairness-aware NLP system development. The discussion focuses on three key areas. First, it outlines methodological principles for designing fairness-sensitive institutional NLP datasets. Second, it proposes evaluation guidelines for discourse-aware benchmarking. Third, it introduces a structured auditing checklist that organisations can use when deploying AI systems in professional communication environments.

Rather than advocating wholesale replacement of existing NLP systems, this chapter positions **benchmarking and evaluation** as core accountability mechanisms that complement human oversight in institutional contexts.

6.2 Reframing Fairness in Institutional NLP

Fairness research in natural language processing has traditionally focused on demographic bias. Studies often examine whether models treat demographic groups differently when predicting sentiment, toxicity, or other classification outcomes. While this work has produced important methodological advances, it does not fully address the fairness challenges that arise in professional communication.

Institutional discourse differs fundamentally from general conversational language. In legal, administrative, and regulatory environments, language performs procedural functions. Questions establish evidentiary claims, hedging expressions signal epistemic uncertainty, and discourse markers organise interactional structure. Errors in these features may alter the interpretation of institutional actions.

The empirical results presented in Chap. 5 demonstrate that fairness disparities often emerge through **pragmatic feature degradation rather than lexical bias**. Models may produce similar classification accuracy across languages while failing to preserve the pragmatic signals that shape institutional meaning.

Consequently, fairness evaluation in institutional NLP must extend beyond demographic parity to include discourse-sensitive criteria. Linguistic equity requires that computational systems preserve not only semantic content but also the pragmatic structures that regulate professional communication.

6.3 Guidelines for Corpus Design

The first requirement for fairness-aware institutional NLP is the availability of appropriate datasets. Many existing NLP benchmarks are derived from general-domain corpora such as news articles or social media. These datasets rarely capture the procedural structure of institutional discourse.

The corpus design principles outlined in Chap. 3 suggest several guidelines for constructing datasets suitable for fairness evaluation.

Domain specificity

Institutional NLP datasets should reflect the communication environments in which systems will be deployed. For legal applications, this includes courtroom questioning, legal documentation, and interpreter-mediated interactions.

Datasets must capture the structural characteristics of these contexts, including regulated turn-taking, evidentiary language, and pragmatic mitigation strategies.

Multilingual representation

Institutional communication frequently occurs across linguistic boundaries. Datasets used for fairness evaluation should therefore include multilingual segments aligned across languages where possible.

Cross-lingual alignment allows researchers to examine whether computational systems preserve pragmatic meaning across languages.

Discourse-level annotation

Traditional NLP annotation schemes often focus on syntactic or lexical information. However, fairness evaluation requires additional annotation layers capturing pragmatic features such as modality, stance markers, and discourse markers.

These annotations enable computational models to represent institutional discourse structures more accurately.

Transparent documentation

To support reproducibility, corpus construction procedures should be documented in detail. Documentation should include data sourcing protocols, anonymisation procedures, annotation guidelines, and reliability measures.

Transparent documentation strengthens the credibility of fairness evaluation results and facilitates replication by other researchers.

6.4 Metric Selection for Fairness Evaluation

A second critical component of fairness-aware institutional NLP is the selection of appropriate evaluation metrics. Conventional classification metrics such as precision, recall, and F1 score provide useful indicators of predictive performance but do not capture discourse-level distortions.

The **Manner Accuracy Score (MAS 2.0)** introduced in Chap. 4 addresses this limitation by combining three components:

semantic accuracy
pragmatic feature retention
discourse function consistency

This composite structure allows researchers to evaluate whether computational outputs preserve the communicative manner in which institutional statements are expressed.

In practical evaluation scenarios, MAS should be used alongside conventional metrics rather than replacing them. Standard metrics remain valuable for measuring baseline predictive performance, while MAS provides additional insight into discourse-sensitive fairness.

Combining these metrics enables a more comprehensive assessment of system behaviour.

6.5 Cross-Lingual Validation Strategies

Multilingual evaluation is essential for assessing fairness in institutional NLP systems. As demonstrated in Chap. 5, performance disparities often emerge when models trained primarily on one language are applied to another. To detect and interpret such disparities systematically, cross-lingual validation should incorporate several complementary evaluation strategies rather than relying on a single performance metric.

First, language-specific benchmarking evaluates model performance separately on datasets representing each language used in institutional communication. This approach enables researchers to identify disparities in baseline accuracy that may remain hidden when performance is aggregated across languages. Second, cross-lingual transfer testing examines whether models trained in one language can generalise to another, providing insight into whether the model captures language-independent discourse structures or relies primarily on language-specific lexical cues. Third, pragmatic equivalence analysis focuses on whether pragmatic features are preserved across aligned multilingual segments. Differences in pragmatic feature retention may indicate fairness risks, particularly when institutional meaning depends on subtle discourse cues such as modality, stance, or mitigation.

These validation strategies provide a comprehensive view of cross-lingual model behaviour and support more reliable fairness assessment in multilingual institutional NLP systems.

6.6 Bias Auditing in Institutional NLP Systems

Beyond experimental evaluation, fairness-aware institutional NLP requires systematic auditing procedures. While model evaluation measures performance under controlled experimental conditions, auditing frameworks monitor system behaviour during deployment and help identify emerging fairness risks in real-world settings. Based on the analyses presented in this Brief, several auditing dimensions are particularly relevant.

One important dimension is pragmatic feature monitoring. Institutional language often relies on discourse markers, hedging expressions, and modality indicators that shape how statements are interpreted. Monitoring whether computational systems detect or preserve these features helps ensure that institutional meaning is not distorted during automated processing. A second dimension concerns error distribution analysis. Rather than aggregating error rates across the entire dataset, auditors should examine performance across different discourse categories, as particular linguistic constructions may generate disproportionate errors.

Additional auditing procedures include cross-lingual parity checks and domain robustness testing. In multilingual environments, system performance should be monitored separately for each language to identify disparities in pragmatic feature retention or discourse classification accuracy. Domain robustness testing further evaluates whether systems maintain consistent behaviour under realistic variation in interaction style, participant roles, or discourse intensity. Together, these auditing procedures help ensure that fairness evaluation reflects the complexity of institutional communication environments.

6.7 A Structured Fairness Auditing Checklist

To facilitate practical implementation, this study proposes a structured auditing checklist for institutional NLP systems. The checklist summarises the evaluation principles developed throughout the book (Table 6.1).

This checklist provides a practical framework for integrating fairness evaluation into institutional NLP development and deployment processes.

Table 6.1 Institutional NLP fairness auditing checklist

Evaluation dimension	Key questions
Corpus representativeness	Does the training dataset reflect the institutional communication domain?
Cross-lingual coverage	Are multiple languages represented in the dataset?
Pragmatic annotation	Are discourse markers, modality, and stance features annotated?
Baseline performance	Do standard metrics (precision, recall, F1) meet acceptable thresholds?
Pragmatic fidelity	Does MAS evaluation show consistent pragmatic feature retention?
Cross-lingual parity	Are MAS scores comparable across languages?
Error distribution	Are errors evenly distributed across discourse categories?

6.8 Human Oversight and Algorithmic Accountability

Although computational evaluation plays an essential role in fairness auditing, it cannot replace human judgement in institutional decision-making. AI systems used in professional contexts should therefore operate within **human-in-the-loop governance structures**.

Human oversight remains critical for several reasons.

First, institutional communication often involves contextual interpretation that exceeds the capabilities of automated systems. Legal professionals, interpreters, and domain experts provide essential expertise in evaluating communicative intent.

Second, fairness concerns may arise in ways that are difficult to quantify computationally. Human review processes can identify subtle interpretive distortions that automated metrics may overlook.

Finally, transparent oversight mechanisms enhance public trust in AI systems used in professional environments. Benchmarking frameworks such as MAS 2.0 should therefore be understood as tools for accountability rather than as substitutes for institutional judgement.

6.9 Future Research Directions

The framework developed in this Brief opens several avenues for future research in fairness-aware institutional NLP.

Multimodal institutional datasets

Institutional communication often includes non-verbal cues such as prosody, gesture, and visual context. Integrating audio and video data into NLP analysis could provide a more comprehensive representation of pragmatic meaning.

Multimodal datasets would enable researchers to examine how linguistic and paralinguistic signals jointly influence institutional interactions.

Large-scale multilingual benchmarking

Current fairness research often relies on relatively small domain-specific datasets. Developing large-scale multilingual institutional corpora would enable more robust benchmarking of fairness-aware NLP systems.

Such initiatives could support cross-disciplinary collaboration among computational linguists, legal scholars, and social scientists.

Explainable discourse modelling

Advances in explainable AI may allow future models to represent institutional discourse structures more transparently. Improved interpretability techniques could help researchers understand how models encode pragmatic features and identify potential sources of bias.

Policy-oriented evaluation frameworks

As AI systems become increasingly integrated into professional environments, policymakers may require formal evaluation standards for fairness-aware NLP. Developing standardised auditing protocols could support responsible AI governance across institutional domains.

6.10 Conclusion

This Brief has examined fairness in AI-mediated institutional communication through the lens of computational sociolinguistics. By integrating discourse analysis with machine learning evaluation, the study developed a framework for operationalising linguistic equity in multilingual professional contexts.

The empirical analyses demonstrated that fairness disparities often arise through pragmatic feature degradation rather than lexical misclassification. Conventional evaluation metrics therefore fail to capture important aspects of institutional communication.

To address this gap, the study introduced the **Manner Accuracy Score (MAS 2.0)** and a transformer-based benchmarking architecture for discourse-sensitive fairness evaluation. Together with the multilingual institutional corpus presented in earlier chapters, these tools provide a methodological foundation for future research in fairness-aware institutional NLP.

More broadly, the findings highlight the importance of integrating sociolinguistic insight into computational system design. Institutional communication is shaped by complex pragmatic structures that cannot be fully captured by general-domain language models.

Ensuring fairness in AI-mediated professional communication therefore requires interdisciplinary collaboration between computational linguistics, sociolinguistics, and institutional governance. By developing evaluation frameworks that reflect the realities of institutional discourse, researchers and practitioners can help ensure that AI systems support rather than undermine equitable communication in professional domains.

References

1. Barocas, S., Hardt, M., Narayanan, A.: Fairness and Machine Learning: Limitations and Opportunities. MIT Press (2019)
2. Floridi, L., Cowls, J.: A unified framework of five principles for AI in society. Harvard Data Sci. Rev. **1**(1) (2019). https://doi.org/10.1162/99608f92.8cd550d1
3. Mehrabi, N., Morstatter, F., Saxena, N., Lerman, K., Galstyan, A.: A survey on bias and fairness in machine learning. ACM Comput. Surv. **54**(6), 1–35 (2021). https://doi.org/10.1145/3457607
4. Alarie, B., Niblett, A., Yoon, A.H.: How artificial intelligence will affect the practice of law. Univ. Toronto Law J. **68**(1), 106–124 (2018). https://doi.org/10.3138/utlj.2017-0052

5. Katz, D.M., Hartung, D., Gerlach, L., Jana, A., Bommarito, M.J., II.: Natural language processing in the legal domain: current status and future directions. Artific. Intell. Law **31**(1), 1–34 (2023). https://doi.org/10.48550/arXiv.2302.12039
6. Bengio, Y., Courville, A., Vincent, P.: Representation learning: A review and new perspectives. IEEE Trans. Pattern Anal. Mach. Intell. **35**(8), 1798–1828 (2013). https://doi.org/10.1109/TPAMI.2013.50
7. Devlin, J., Chang, M.-W., Lee, K., Toutanova, K.: BERT: pre-training of deep bidirectional transformers for language understanding. In: Proceedings of NAACL 2019, pp. 4171–4186. Association for Computational Linguistics (2019). https://doi.org/10.18653/v1/N19-1423.
8. Gallegos, I.O., Rossi, R.A., Barrow, J., Tanjim, M.M., Kim, S., Dernoncourt, F., Yu, T., Zhang, R., Ahmed, N.K.: Bias and fairness in large language models: a survey. Comput. Linguist. **50**(3), 1097–1179 (2024). https://doi.org/10.1162/coli_a_00524

Chapter 7
Conclusion: Toward Fairness-Aware NLP in Professional Domains

Keywords Fairness-aware NLP · Institutional AI systems · Multilingual professional communication · Linguistic equity in AI · Discourse-sensitive evaluation · AI governance and accountability

7.1 Introduction

Artificial intelligence is increasingly embedded in institutional communication infrastructures. Systems based on large language models and transformer architectures now support tasks such as legal document analysis, multilingual translation, professional writing assistance, and evidence processing. These developments offer substantial efficiency gains but also introduce new risks. When computational systems mediate professional discourse, errors or distortions may influence credibility assessments, evidentiary interpretation, and procedural outcomes. For this reason, evaluating fairness in AI-mediated institutional communication has become a critical research and governance challenge.

Recent developments in legal informatics and computational law demonstrate how AI technologies are reshaping professional decision-making processes, particularly in domains such as legal analytics, document review, and regulatory compliance [1–3]. At the same time, scholarship on responsible AI governance highlights the need for transparent evaluation frameworks capable of detecting bias and unintended social consequences in algorithmic systems deployed within institutional settings [4, 5].

In natural language processing research, transformer-based architectures have dramatically expanded the capacity of AI systems to model complex linguistic patterns [6, 7]. However, recent studies have shown that even highly capable models may exhibit systematic biases or distortions when applied to specialised domains such as legal or institutional communication [8, 9]. These findings highlight the

© The Author(s), under exclusive license to Springer Nature Switzerland AG 2026
R. Yi et al., *Algorithmic Fairness in AI-Mediated Institutional Communication*, SpringerBriefs in Computer Science, https://doi.org/10.1007/978-3-032-28658-1_7

importance of developing evaluation frameworks that account for the structural properties of professional discourse rather than relying solely on general-purpose NLP benchmarks.

This Brief addressed that challenge by developing a computational framework for evaluating **linguistic equity in multilingual institutional communication systems**. The central research question guiding the study was how fairness in professional discourse can be operationalised, measured, and benchmarked using transformer-based NLP architectures. Across the preceding chapters, the analysis combined sociolinguistic theory, corpus design, and computational modelling to produce a reproducible framework for discourse-sensitive fairness evaluation.

This concluding chapter synthesises the theoretical and empirical contributions of the Brief. It first summarises the conceptual framework developed throughout the study. It then highlights the methodological contributions and key empirical findings. Finally, it discusses the broader implications of fairness-aware NLP for professional domains and outlines directions for future research.

7.2 From Sociolinguistic Theory to Computational Evaluation

A central premise of this work is that fairness in institutional communication cannot be assessed solely through demographic bias metrics or aggregate classification accuracy. Institutional discourse is governed by procedural norms that regulate interactional roles, evidentiary language, and pragmatic signalling. Linguistic form therefore plays a critical role in shaping professional interactions.

Chapter 2 translated these sociolinguistic insights into computational constructs. Concepts such as pragmatic appropriateness, discourse alignment, and communicative accountability were operationalised as measurable features within computational models. This theoretical translation provided the foundation for evaluating linguistic equity in institutional NLP systems.

The framework introduced in this Brief conceptualises fairness across three analytical layers:

Discourse-level competence, referring to the ability of computational systems to capture pragmatic features embedded in professional communication.
Model-level performance parity, referring to consistent predictive performance across languages and discourse categories.
System-level accountability, referring to the interpretability and governance of AI systems deployed in institutional contexts.

Together, these layers define a multidimensional understanding of fairness that extends beyond conventional machine learning metrics.

7.3 Building an Empirical Foundation for Institutional NLP

Operationalising fairness in institutional communication requires domain-specific data. Chapter 3 addressed this requirement by introducing a multilingual institutional corpus constructed from two complementary sources: a prosecutorial questioning dataset and a bilingual courtroom interpreting dataset derived from simulated criminal trials.

The corpus was designed to capture pragmatic features that play a central role in institutional discourse. Annotation layers included polarity alignment, stance markers, modality, hedging expressions, and discourse markers. Inter-annotator reliability analysis confirmed strong agreement for discourse-function classification, ensuring that the dataset provides a robust empirical basis for computational modelling.

In addition to linguistic annotation, the corpus design incorporated procedures for anonymisation, preprocessing, and cross-lingual alignment. These steps ensure that the dataset can support reproducible computational experiments while protecting participant confidentiality.

By integrating discourse analysis with multilingual data preparation, the corpus provides an empirical foundation for fairness-aware benchmarking in institutional NLP.

7.4 Transformer-Based Benchmarking for Institutional Discourse

Building on this empirical foundation, Chap. 4 introduced a transformer-based benchmarking architecture designed to evaluate fairness in institutional NLP systems. The framework combines multilingual transformer fine-tuning with discourse-sensitive evaluation metrics.

The benchmarking architecture includes several key components:

multilingual transformer encoding of institutional discourse
supervised classification of discourse functions
feature attribution analysis for interpretability
cross-lingual transfer evaluation
domain robustness testing

Most importantly, the chapter introduced the **Manner Accuracy Score (MAS 2.0)** as a discourse-aware evaluation metric. MAS extends traditional performance measures by incorporating pragmatic feature retention and discourse-function consistency alongside semantic accuracy.

This metric reflects the insight that fairness in professional communication depends not only on what systems predict but also on **how institutional meaning is represented**.

7.5 Empirical Evidence of Discourse-Level Fairness Disparities

Chapter 5 applied the benchmarking framework to evaluate fairness and bias in AI-mediated institutional communication systems. The analysis revealed several important patterns.

First, cross-lingual evaluation showed that baseline classification accuracy remained relatively stable across English and Mandarin datasets. However, when pragmatic feature retention was incorporated through MAS evaluation, larger disparities became visible.

Second, error distribution analysis demonstrated that model errors clustered around specific pragmatic constructions, particularly polarity reversal tags and epistemic stance markers. These constructions are central to adversarial courtroom questioning and play a key role in shaping interactional dynamics.

Third, domain shift experiments showed that pragmatic fidelity is more sensitive to contextual variation than lexical classification accuracy. Models trained in one institutional context exhibited performance degradation when applied to another.

Taken together, these findings indicate that fairness disparities in institutional NLP systems often arise through **pragmatic signal degradation rather than explicit lexical bias**. This result underscores the importance of discourse-sensitive evaluation methods.

7.6 Implications for Fairness-Aware NLP Design

The framework developed in this Brief has several practical implications for the design and evaluation of NLP systems used in professional domains.

Domain-sensitive evaluation

Institutional communication involves linguistic structures that differ from those found in general language corpora. Evaluating AI systems using domain-specific benchmarks is therefore essential for detecting fairness risks.

Multilingual validation

Cross-lingual testing should be a standard component of fairness evaluation in institutional NLP systems. Models trained primarily on one language may fail to capture equivalent pragmatic structures in other languages.

Discourse-aware metrics

Evaluation metrics must account for pragmatic features embedded in institutional discourse. Metrics such as MAS provide a mechanism for measuring whether computational systems preserve the communicative manner in which professional statements are expressed.

Interpretability and transparency

Fairness auditing requires interpretability tools capable of identifying the linguistic features driving model predictions. Feature attribution analysis allows researchers and practitioners to diagnose fairness issues and improve system design.

These principles collectively support the development of more reliable and accountable NLP systems for professional communication environments.

7.7 Benchmarking as an Accountability Mechanism

A key conclusion of this study is that fairness-aware benchmarking should be viewed as an **accountability mechanism rather than a purely technical evaluation exercise**. Institutional NLP systems operate within governance structures that include legal standards, professional norms, and ethical obligations.

Benchmarking frameworks provide empirical tools for evaluating whether computational systems meet these standards. By identifying disparities in pragmatic fidelity, cross-lingual performance, and discourse interpretation, benchmarking helps ensure that AI systems do not inadvertently distort institutional communication.

Importantly, benchmarking does not replace human oversight. Instead, it complements human expertise by providing systematic evidence about model behaviour. Legal professionals, interpreters, and institutional stakeholders remain essential participants in evaluating the consequences of AI-mediated communication.

7.8 Toward Fairness-Aware NLP in Professional Domains

The increasing adoption of AI systems in professional environments makes fairness-aware NLP research both timely and necessary. Institutional communication plays a central role in legal decision-making, regulatory compliance, and professional collaboration. Ensuring that computational systems support equitable communication is therefore a matter of both technical reliability and institutional legitimacy.

The framework developed in this Brief contributes to this objective by integrating sociolinguistic theory with computational evaluation methods. By operationalising linguistic equity as a measurable property of NLP systems, the study demonstrates how fairness can be evaluated in multilingual professional contexts.

Future research will benefit from expanding this approach to additional institutional domains. Potential directions include healthcare communication, regulatory compliance analysis, and international administrative cooperation. Developing larger multilingual institutional corpora and multimodal datasets incorporating audio and visual signals will further strengthen fairness evaluation.

Advances in explainable AI may also improve our ability to understand how computational models represent pragmatic structures in professional discourse. Such developments could enable more transparent auditing of AI systems used in high-stakes environments.

7.9 Final Remarks

The rapid expansion of AI-mediated communication technologies presents both opportunities and challenges for professional domains. While transformer-based language models have dramatically improved the capabilities of NLP systems, their deployment in institutional contexts requires careful evaluation of fairness and accountability.

This Brief has argued that fairness in institutional NLP cannot be reduced to demographic parity or classification accuracy. Instead, fairness must be understood as the preservation of linguistic structures that shape institutional meaning and procedural interaction.

By combining discourse analysis, multilingual corpus design, and transformer-based benchmarking, this study offers a methodological pathway toward fairness-aware NLP systems capable of supporting equitable communication in professional environments.

As AI continues to reshape the infrastructures of institutional communication, developing such frameworks will remain an essential task for researchers, practitioners, and policymakers alike.

References

1. Alarie, B., Niblett, A., Yoon, A.H.: Regulation by machine. In: Proceedings of the 30th Conference on Neural Information Processing Systems (2016). https://doi.org/10.2139/ssrn.2878950.
2. Ariai, F., Mackenzie, J., Demartini, G.: Natural language processing for the legal domain: a survey of tasks, datasets, models, and challenges. ACM Comput. Surv. **58**(6), 1–37 (2025). https://doi.org/10.1145/3777009
3. Katz, D.M., Hartung, D., Gerlach, L., Jana, A., Bommarito, M.J., II.: Natural language processing in the legal domain: Current status and future directions. Artific. Intell. Law **31**(1), 1–34 (2023). https://doi.org/10.48550/arXiv.2302.12039
4. Caton, S., Haas, C.: Fairness in machine learning: a survey. ACM Comput. Surv. (2024). https://doi.org/10.1145/3616865

5. Floridi, L., Cowls, J.: A unified framework of five principles for AI in society. Harvard Data Sci. Rev. **1**(1) (2019). https://doi.org/10.1162/99608f92.8cd550d1
6. Devlin, J., Chang, M.-W., Lee, K., Toutanova, K.: BERT: pre-training of deep bidirectional transformers for language understanding. In: Proceedings of NAACL 2019, pp. 4171–4186. Association for Computational Linguistics (2019). https://doi.org/10.18653/v1/N19-1423.
7. Vaswani, A., Shazeer, N., Parmar, N., Uszkoreit, J., Jones, L., Gomez, A. N., Kaiser, Ł., Polosukhin, I.: Attention is all you need. In: Advances in Neural Information Processing Systems, vol. 30, pp. 5998–6008 (2017). URL https://proceedings.neurips.cc/paper/2017/hash/3f5ee243547dee91fbd053c1c4a845aa-Abstract.html.
8. Blodgett, S.L., Barocas, S., Daumé III, H., Wallach, H.: Language (technology) is power: a critical survey of bias in NLP. In: Proceedings of the 58th Annual Meeting of the Association for Computational Linguistics, pp. 5454–5476. Association for Computational Linguistics (2020). https://doi.org/10.18653/v1/2020.acl-main.485.
9. Gallegos, I.O., Rossi, R.A., Barrow, J., Tanjim, M.M., Kim, S., Dernoncourt, F., Yu, T., Zhang, R., Ahmed, N.K.: Bias and fairness in large language models: a survey. Comput. Linguist. **50**(3), 1097–1179 (2024). https://doi.org/10.1162/coli_a_00524

MIX
Papier aus verantwortungsvollen Quellen
Paper from responsible sources
FSC® C105338

If you have any concerns about our products,
you can contact us on
ProductSafety@springernature.com

In case Publisher is established outside the EU,
the EU authorized representative is:
Springer Nature Customer Service Center GmbH
Europaplatz 3, 69115 Heidelberg, Germany

Printed by Libri Plureos GmbH
in Hamburg, Germany